Ethics After Aristotle

Based on the Carl Newell Jackson Lectures

Ethics After Aristotle

BRAD INWOOD

Harvard University Press

Cambridge, Massachusetts
London, England
2014

Library of Congress Cataloging-in-Publication Data
Inwood, Brad.
Ethics after Aristotle / Brad Inwood.
p.   cm
Includes bibliographical references and index.
ISBN 978-0-674-73125-7 (alk. paper)
I. Ethics, Ancient.   2. Aristotle—Influence.   I. Title.
BJ161.I59 2014
170.938—dc23   2013040261

To the memory of Steven Michael Inwood (1956–2011)

Mentem mortalia tangunt

Contents

Preface   ix

1. Working in the Wake of Genius   I

2. Flirting with Hedonism (It's Only Natural)   30

3. The Turning Point: From Critolaus to Cicero   51

4. Bridging the Gap: Aristotelian Ethics in the
   Early Roman Empire   73

5. Alexander and Imperial Aristotelianism   105

Notes   127
Note on the Ancient Texts   147
Bibliography   149
Source Index   157
Subject Index   161

Preface

The lectures on which this short book is based were delivered at Harvard University in April of 2011, at the invitation of the Department of the Classics. I am grateful to the department and especially to Professor Kathleen Coleman for the honor and for the opportunity to develop these thoughts in a more organized way than I had been able to do previously. I am grateful to the audience for stimulating questions and challenges. I owe a particular debt to Gisela Striker, for her interventions on the occasion of the lectures, for the example of her incomparable work on ancient ethics, and for a supportive philosophical friendship that spans more than a quarter century. At a later stage I benefitted a great deal from presenting parts of this project to the ancient philosophy community at the University of California at Berkeley; their vigorous discussion contributed to a number of significant improvements in the argument.

My deepest gratitude, though, goes to two of my colleagues at the University of Toronto, John Magee and Jennifer Whiting. Both of them read the lectures as they were being developed and provided a helpful balance of criticism and encouragement, though neither has read the final version and only I am responsible for any mistakes or confusions which persist. John and Jennifer are ideal colleagues and collaborators, embodying the contrasting excellences that define the field of ancient philosophy, John on the historical-philological side and Jennifer on the philosophical side. In a field that cannot afford to neglect either approach, the examples they provide are never far from my mind and their friendship is never absent from my thoughts.

I would also like to acknowledge here the financial support of the Social Sciences and Humanities Research Council of Canada and the Canada Research Chairs program of the Canadian government. The Departments of Philosophy and Classics at the University of Toronto have also provided unstinting support for my work over the years.

It is with sadness that I dedicate this book to the memory of my brother, Steven Michael Inwood, whose illness and premature death have dominated my thoughts as these lectures were written, delivered, and revised. He touched and inspired all who knew him, for however short or long a time. Solon and Aristotle agreed that we can deem no one's life a success until it is over, and Steve's life was indeed a great success; his life as a whole was an activity in accordance with excellences of the human soul. He was *eudaimōn*, but the pain we feel at losing him so young is not thereby assuaged.

I

Working in the Wake of Genius

Aristotle has always been a hard act to follow. His philosophical and scientific achievements spanned a wide range of disciplines, many of which he could easily claim to have founded. In the fields to which he devoted his principal efforts, his breadth of vision, acuity, and good judgment set a standard which lasted for centuries. And in the fields in which he did little work himself—I am thinking of mathematics and astronomy, musical theory, medicine, mechanics, and geography— Aristotle proved to be strikingly well informed and often provided an articulated framework for investigation and explanation that served as a guide for others. This book is about the impact of Aristotle's achievement in ethics, but it won't hurt to begin with an acknowledgement that his genius cast a very long shadow over many fields—logic, semantics, rhetoric, dialectic, cosmology, natural philosophy, biology (or, more precisely, zoology), psychology and epistemology, meta-physics (both high and low, the study of the best and most distinctive form of being and also the most finely grained analysis of all beings),

I

cultural and literary history, political theory. . . . The list could go on, of course, but even when it does it won't include botany, and theology will have to be taken as a special case. As we all know, Aristotle's own theories about god didn't connect well with the intuitions and prior commitments of his culture and it was a long time until his contributions could be brought back into serious dialogue with other theologies, whether philosophical or not.

Whether you think of coming along after such a figure as standing in his shadow or on his shoulders, the historical situation is distinctive. Without, I hope, falling prey to the usual clichés about *epigoni,* we can surely recognize a pattern in the history of many intellectual and cultural disciplines. After the "great man," then what? In our understanding of the history of philosophy we have long acknowledged the situation: it would be useful, though tedious, to catalogue all the post-thises and neo-thats which mark our awareness that unusually powerful and influential thinkers leave a recognizable wake in the generations which follow them (and which inevitably go on to do their own work).

My purpose in these chapters, as it was in the lectures they are based on, is to conduct a preliminary exploration of the aftermath of Aristotelian ethics.[1] There are several reasons for focusing on ethics. First, it is a field which Aristotle founded *as a discipline.* I don't mean to claim that no one had indulged in constructive (or destructive) thought about ethics before Aristotle, any more than one would claim that no one had indulged in structured reasoning or reflected on it before Aristotle founded logic. But as with logic, Aristotle was the first to set relatively clear boundaries to the field of ethics, to identify with some precision high-level principles that define it and provide a framework for working within it, and to make distinctive claims about the field which have had enduring importance. Plato and others had of course said a great deal about ethics, but whereas Plato left the relationship

of ethics to metaphysics complicated and murky, Aristotle successfully isolated it and wrote at least two distinct treatises on ethics and
thereby established a new genre of philosophical writing. One might
think, as some Platonists certainly did, that ethics is ill served by being
so sharply distinguished from metaphysics; or that Aristotle underesti-
mated the importance and intimacy of the relationship between ethics
and politics; or that ethics needs to be more tightly connected to an
understanding of human biology and psychology than even Aristotle
realized. But there is no denying that it was Aristotle's example and
influence that made ethics into the distinct discipline it still is. His
contemporary and sometime rival Xenocrates first divided philosophy
tidily into three fields, physics, logic, and ethics.[2] But it was Aristotle
who made ethics a field of its own.

But a much stronger motivation for choosing to focus on ethics
is the enduring importance of Aristotle's approach to the subject.
His *Nicomachean Ethics* has been the most consistently studied treatise
in the history of ethics; it has done more than any other text to give
the field whatever unity and cohesion it has. Beyond that, in the last
generation or two an approach to ethical enquiry which owes explicit
allegiance to Aristotle has come onto the scene. In the nearly six
decades years since Elizabeth Anscombe's "Modern Moral Philosophy"[3] and largely as a result of her stimulus[4] something recognizable
as an Aristotelian approach to ethics has re-emerged alongside of and
as a challenge to what had been, in the mid twentieth century, the
two main approaches to the subject. What we now typically regard
as the deontological approach to ethics (an approach whose practi-
tioners typically look to Kant as inspiration) and what Anscombe
herself (op.cit. p. 12) dubbed "consequentialism" were then dominant and were thought to exhaust the field of plausible approaches
to ethics. For Anscombe, as for a large and still growing group of

moral philosophers, Aristotle's ethics represents a distinct approach to the subject, one that promises a way forward on many problems which seemed intractable or unresolvable in the framework of the mid twentieth century. "Virtue ethics" is the most familiar tag for this movement, but it also bears the label "neo-Aristotelian," and not without reason. One of the questions which I will be asking is this: what is it that most properly characterizes an approach to moral theory as Aristotelian? But I will be asking the question in the historical context of ancient philosophy: what most properly characterized an *ancient* moral theory as Aristotelian?

For a relatively uncontroversial account of why an Aristotelian approach still matters, I turn to a familiar authority: the opening paragraphs of Rosalynd Hursthouse's article on "Virtue Ethics" in the *Stanford Encyclopedia of Philosophy*. According to Hursthouse, when virtue ethics emerged in Anscombe's article, it

> crystallised an increasing dissatisfaction with the forms of deontology and utilitarianism then prevailing. Neither of them, at that time, paid attention to a number of topics that had always figured in the virtue ethics tradition—the virtues themselves, motives and moral character, moral education, moral wisdom or discernment, friendship and family relationships, a deep concept of happiness, the role of the emotions in our moral life and the fundamentally important questions of what sort of person I should be and how we should live. . . .
>
> But although modern virtue ethics does not have to take the form known as "neo-Aristotelian," almost any modern version still shows that its roots are in ancient Greek philosophy by the employment of three concepts derived from it. These are *aretē* (excellence or virtue), *phronēsis* (practical or moral wisdom), and *eudaimonia* (usually translated as happiness or flourishing).[5]

Hursthouse also points out that neo-Aristotelianism has been a useful stimulus in many areas of contemporary moral philosophy. This has produced a renewed motivation for the study of Aristotle's ethics, in the first instance the *Nicomachean Ethics* (*NE*), which has had the greatest historical impact, though appreciation for the contribution of his other major treatise on ethics, the *Eudemian Ethics* (*EE*), is growing.[6] But despite the short list of relevant Aristotelian themes supplied by Hursthouse, it is by no means clear what it is that warrants calling this strain in moral theory "Aristotelian" or "neo-Aristotelian."

Simply talking about virtue, practical wisdom, and happiness is not enough to make an ethics Aristotelian; others besides Aristotelians embraced those themes, as a study of the wider ancient eudaimonist tradition confirms.[7] Nor is it clear that contemporary neo-Aristotelianism uniformly embraces several other features of Aristotle's own moral theory which are often thought to characterize it. Here I am thinking of the role played by *activities* alongside *dispositions* (the good life is an *energeia* of some very particular human dispositions), the central place of friendship,[8] a preoccupation with the analysis of various kinds of goods and their role in the happy life, and a detailed analysis of the phenomena pertinent to moral psychology—all of which are correctly identified as salient aspects of his theory. So, if much of what contemporary moral theorists regard as Aristotelian was shared by other schools in the ancient world and if much of what was distinctive of Aristotle's own moral theory is not in fact routinely embraced by modern neo-Aristotelians, then we evidently do need to ask what it is that is supposed to make a theory Aristotelian in the first place.

It will perhaps help to recognize that neo-Aristotelianism in ethics is both much older and more complex than is currently appreciated. Versions of Aristotelian ethical theory have been revived repeatedly in the western tradition, the most influential such revival before the twentieth century being its transformation by Thomas Aquinas. But long before that Aristotle's own followers, the Peripatetics, also developed innovative contributions to moral theory along broadly Aristotelian lines. My plan is to bring these ancient neo-Aristotelians into the story, to draw on their philosophical innovations to help us achieve a fuller grasp of what in the end has been distinctively and persistently Aristotelian about neo-Aristotelian ethics and of how we can best use it today.[9]

It is worthwhile to anticipate one of the key features of the account that I will be offering. Although, as I have indicated, one of the most currently influential features of Aristotelian ethics derives from his account of the role of the virtues in a good human life—Aristotle really is, in a way, the founding father of virtue ethics—I will be directing far more of my attention to what I am referring to as his naturalism, to the distinctively Aristotelian view that we learn more about ethics and human happiness by focusing on our relationship to nature than by analyzing the particular virtues recognized in our own (or any other particular) culture. I should perhaps digress a bit to explain why.

The complicated role played by virtue in Aristotle's ethics was outlined synoptically and economically by Crisp and Slote in the introduction to their 1997 collection *Virtue Ethics*,[10] but the basic insight is relatively simple. We are urged to follow Aristotle's example and organize our moral theory around the notion of human virtues or excellences rather than around more "abstract" concepts such as utility or duty. On this approach, we are to focus on living according to the virtues and to look, as Aristotle did, to the achievement of a good life in that sense as the reference point of moral theory. We may or may not find it easy to agree on what the virtues actually are or on their relative importance, but that is where the main debate is supposed to be focused.

But Aristotelian ethics is also supposed to be a model for a kind of ethical naturalism. In *Nicomachean Ethics* I.7 Aristotle notoriously deploys something called the "function argument," which claims that human beings, like other animals, have natural functions, the fulfillment of which constitutes their *telos,* their success conditions as living things—and the achievement of that success condition for humans bears the label "happiness" or *eudaimonia.*[11] (The situation is similar for many tools and artifacts, though their function is established by us rather than by nature; that is why they make such clear and useful analogies.) And our function, like that of other animals (and plants as well, perhaps), is rooted in our nature, a set of essential and defining traits whose presence and relevance in our lives is taken to be not open to debate. It is our nature that makes us what we are, and in Aristotle's teleological view of the natural world it simply doesn't make sense to ask *why* one would want to fulfill one's function, what the goodness of doing so would be, or how to justify a living life according to one's nature. As Philippa Foot,[12] perhaps the most influential exponent of this general view, puts it, there is "no change in the meaning of 'good' between the word as it appears in 'good roots' and as it appears in 'good dispositions of the human will.'"[13] Goodness in human moral terms and goodness in any relevant biological application stand in the same relationship to the nature of the species in question. With or without the refined account of how this is metaphysically rooted, which Michael Thompson provides in *Life and Action*[14] (using a theory of "Aristotelian" natural-historical "categoricals"), this provides a powerful challenge to other accounts of what human goodness consists in. If it works, it constitutes a kind of preemptive strike against nonnaturalist theories. For if the evaluative preferability of (say) various prosocial behaviors can be explained successfully as a function of our species' natural makeup, then explanation in terms of anything more complicated or posterior (such as a debatable conception of utility or some contentious notion of unconditional goodness) will be otiose and to that extent intellectually unattractive.

These two aspects of Aristotelian ethics from which contemporary moral theory is thought to benefit stand in an interesting relationship.[15] Clearly they are independent of each other in principle. One could argue for the centrality of the virtues in moral evaluation while rejecting naturalism of any kind. The virtues we might put at the center of our theory could be defined by a nonnatural prescriptive theory (think here of the theological virtues); or they could be those recognized in and by a particular culture, virtues which we would learn about largely by gathering information about and reflection on the relevant society and from an analysis of its stable practices of praising and blaming, rewarding and punishing. And such virtues could be significantly different in different societies and subcultures. The courage of a Spartan may not be the courage of an Athenian; the generosity of a contemporary Russian plutocrat may well differ from that of the Ethiopian peasant farmer (which of these would be more like the "generosity" Aristotle recognized in his own world or we in ours is a question I think better left unasked). Of course, it is also possible that there would be human universals to be found among such culturally determined virtues, but the way to discover them would be inductive, by a bottom-up procedure of analysis seeking commonalities among superficially different norms. Universality across our species or across the centuries could not be taken for granted and would certainly not be criterial. It would be the effectively functioning norms in a given society which determine what counts as a virtue. Natural teleology need not come into it.

And conversely, a theory of natural goodness need not generate a set of norms and values for human beings which maps at all well onto any of our favorite normative theories or onto the actual functioning of known societies that *we* happen to approve of. Many of us would no doubt hope that an acute understanding of the nature of our species might explain the apparent value of generosity and courage; and there is no doubt at all in my mind that the desire to get human nature to match up to familiar virtues has at times distorted the attempt to analyze dispassionately just exactly what our nature is. Conventional reactions to some conclusions drawn by sociobiologists reveal the tension. If it starts to look as though manly courage naturally includes the imperative to kill off the male offspring of one's competitors, or as though generosity to the less fortunate is a form of high-minded foolishness (as Callicles might put it), then many a philosopher will urge us to go back to the drawing board (or to redo our ethological field work) until we get a more acceptable answer about human nature.

At this point in our reflections it will be helpful to recall how Aristotle begins the *Nicomachean Ethics*. He deploys the notion, used throughout his works, that things and activities have natural goals. "Every art and enquiry, and similarly every action and decision, is thought to aim at some good; that is why people are right to think that the good is that at which all things aim." We should first and foremost note the universal claim about goal-directedness, which is an instance of the general feature that I am treating as a mark of naturalism—the idea that humans operate according to the same general principles that other parts of the natural world, in particular animals, operate on and so should be evaluated by standards that are at least analogically the same. But we should also note the role played in this passage by people's *beliefs*. Aristotle self-consciously gives an important, even weakly criterial role in thinking through ethical questions to views that were widely held in his culture or held distinctively by its leading intellects. But he also regards human beings (whose goals and activities are the subject matter of ethics) as parts of nature, sophisticated and special animals but animals nonetheless. The relationship between these aspects of his ethics is in principle somewhat unclear.

His naturalism provides Aristotle with one of the most powerful bits of his moral theory—the definition in *NE* I.7 of happiness (or human flourishing) as a pattern of activities, activations of capacities that are characteristic of human nature—human nature being, essentially, our soul, and our soul being, essentially, a set of capacities or capabilities. This is a feature of thriving and success which we share with every natural entity in the world—where "natural" simply means "having a set of *internal* capacities" or "principles of motion and rest." We will soon see that on many issues Aristotle's ethics contains some open-endedness and indeterminacy which his followers will explore, but on this fundamental question (what is happiness?) we can already detect a basic tension. Widely held views (the *endoxa*) also matter and some of them—such as the idea that there are three basic ways of life for humans (devoted to pleasure, honor, or knowledge), all of which deserve their due—play a critical role in defining what counts as human excellence. How these views, or indeed the further notion that there is something basically godlike about the best human life, relate to the natural functions of our species can be a bit of a mystery.

The theoretical independence of Aristotelian virtue ethics (and the attention to commonly held views that underpins it) and Aristotelian naturalism leaves the contemporary Aristotelian sympathizer with a potential dilemma. Unless he or she simply begs the question about human nature, assuming that something recognizable as a genuine virtue just has to be the expression of human nature as *properly* understood, these two aspects of Aristotelianism may well come apart in the context of contemporary debate. And yet our philosophical hero, Aristotle himself, clearly thought of this risk as being negligible or even as nonexistent. For example, he took it as self-evident that man is a naturally social animal—and more than that, that man is a naturally *polis*-dwelling animal. Not only is human nature essentially prosocial, so that anticommunitarian traits of character will be ruled out on principle as candidates for being virtues, but human nature is just as essentially *polis*-bound in Aristotle's view. And a Greek *polis* is the natural home of some quite specific virtues, some of which are foreign enough from our own that the troublesome issue of historical or cultural relativism emerges almost immediately.

It is, or should be, clear to us that there is a real risk of having these two aspects of Aristotelian ethics, each attractive in its own way and for its own reasons, come apart from each other or even come into conflict with each other. And there is also a real prospect that preventing this conflict might come at the price of question-begging apologetics. This would not be a particularly appealing situation to find oneself in. And so it may be that the contributions of Aristotelian ethics to the contemporary setting are better left separate from each other, no matter how tightly Aristotle himself thought they were connected. We have virtue ethics on the one hand and a form of teleological naturalism on the other, and we may set aside the question of whether they are reliably compatible with each other.

We return, then, to the question: what does the virtue-ethical strand of Aristotle's work offer us today? After all, much of what contemporary moral theorists regard as Aristotelian is shared by other schools in the ancient world, and much of what was important in Aristotle's own moral theory is not in fact routinely highlighted by modern neo-Aristotelians. Perhaps the grand vogue of Aristotelianism in recent ethical theorizing is nothing more than a run of enthusiasm for the ancients generally, a reaction, perhaps, against the dominant role played by movements in ethics stemming from the early modern period, from the Enlightenment, and from themes that became dominant due to the influence of Christianity on ethics as practiced in the European tradition. And if Aristotle was a highly visible point of entry for ancient Greco-Roman ethics into twentieth century debates, that is all to the good—but it does not mean that he remains a vital resource for continuing discussion, rather than (say) the Epicureans, Stoics, or anyone else from the history of western philosophical ethics.

Moreover, we may wonder what more Aristotle's virtue ethics in its own right can offer us. It seems to me that virtually all of the inspiration we are going to get from Aristotle has been absorbed. Already we pay close attention to the virtues—although we don't, or at least shouldn't, in my view, worry too much about Aristotle's particular set of virtues; we are accustomed to consider the merits of Aristotle's approach to practical reason (shared to a great extent with Plato and the Stoics) and deliberation (where Aristotle shines with his own brilliant light) alongside Kantian and utilitarian models of how to use reason in guiding human life; I think we more or less take it for granted that a serious contender in moral theory should have something plausible and constructive to say about moral psychology, voluntary agency, and weakness of will. I am not quite so confident that we do in fact expect every respectable moral theory to say something sensible about the role of friendship or contemplation in a properly lived life; equally, I am not at all sure myself that we should expect this of every moral theory. The issue, at any rate, has been on offer in a highly visible place for quite some time now, and those not interested in sampling the wares surely know or ought to know what they are missing.

In short, I think there is a very good argument to be made that Aristotle's ethics has taught contemporary philosophical ethics all that it is likely to teach us for the foreseeable future. Maybe it is a victim of its own success, a success achieved so brilliantly in the last few decades that it no longer seems novel, let alone revolutionary. The degree to which Aristotle's influence has been absorbed on the contemporary scene is perhaps best indicated by some of John McDowell's work. Though rooted deeply in Aristotle, some of McDowell's principal contributions have been highly creative reworkings of his Aristotelian inspiration; I think this is a fair description of, for example, "Two Sorts of Naturalism" (McDowell 1998) and of his complicated mediation between Kant and Aristotle in "Deliberation and Moral Development in Aristotle's Ethics" (McDowell 1996). Indeed, they would *have* to be creative rethinkings of Aristotle in order to preserve their relevance in fast-moving debates which must involve crossing swords with Kantians and fiercely motivated consequentialists. Aristotle never faced either kind of opponent, so it is no wonder that one has to rework his ethics in order to find (or construct) the Aristotelian contribution. Virtue ethics is a mature tradition of its own and does not need its founding father any more. It's not that we won't strengthen our philosophical skills by spending more time thinking with one of the great philosophers of European history; but if we plan to engage on the battlefield of contemporary debate, we probably have by now all the content we need from Aristotle, at least from what he has to say about virtue.

Because of these worries, and perhaps even more because, in my view, virtue ethics, however much it owed to Aristotelianism in getting itself off the ground in the twentieth century, is now a more or less autonomous strand in moral theory, I will be focusing on Aristotelian naturalism in the pages which follow. This will help us to see what was actually characteristic of this tradition since, as I have noted, Aristotle's focus on the virtues and their relationship to happiness and moral success is not in the least distinctive of his work or that of his later followers.

From Aristotle's immediate successor, Theophrastus, all the way to the great Aristotelian commentator Alexander of Aphrodisias in the late second and early third centuries CE, philosophers who understood themselves to be Aristotelians and who drew their ultimate inspiration from his work in ethics were active participants in the evolving ethical debates of their day. For over 500 years Aristotelian moral philosophers in the ancient world put forward new theories, responded to challenges from other schools of thought, interpreted and criticized the work of their founder,[16] and developed a large and varied body of moral theory. They did so in response to perceived weaknesses and puzzles in Aristotle's theory, in awareness that social and political changes required adaptations in substantive moral theory, and in dialogue with the "competition"—the other principal proponents of broadly eudaimonistic theories. These competing theories emerged from the Platonic and Academic tradition, from Stoicism, and even from the hedonistic version of eudaimonism developed in the Epicurean school.[17]

Throughout this long history of debate and change, something recognizably Aristotelian was always present, beyond the kind of loyalty to the name and position of the "founder" which characterizes many ancient philosophical schools for much of their history.[18] No matter how important the role of the founder was in providing institutional and intellectual cohesion to a school (and this varied among schools and across time, with Aristotelianism perhaps least consistently affected until the time of Alexander), there were always *philosophical* reasons for maintaining or adopting a particular school identification. Despite the work of Julia Annas in the *Morality of Happiness* (1993),[19] of Paul Moraux in *Der Aristotelismus bei den Griechen* (1973–2001), of Hans Gottschalk in a major study published in 1987, and of the late Robert Sharples in a wide range of scholarly studies spanning his whole career, it is not yet sufficiently clear what provided the philosophical unity of that ancient Aristotelian tradition.

One indication of this is the following. Cicero famously claimed[20] that it is the understanding of the *telos* (or *summum bonum*) that determines one's fundamental philosophical commitments and affiliations. But the example of ancient neo-Aristotelians proves him wrong. Some few were hedonists; others cheerfully omitted the role of activity in the good life; there was disagreement about the importance of virtue relative to other goods. All of these innovations affect one's understanding of the *telos*. And yet the neo-Aristotelians who held these diverse views thought of themselves as part of a unified tradition, and were right to do so.

The best way I can think of to make progress on the problem is to study in some detail and with primarily philosophical interests in mind the ancient neo-Aristotelian tradition from the time of Theophrastus to the age of Alexander of Aphrodisias. This is now possible to a degree that it was not before, thanks to the great volume of detailed historical and exegetical work undertaken in the last forty years. An improved understanding of the moral theories of the "competition" during the Hellenistic period has also been crucial to preparing the ground for such a study, as is emerging work on Greco-Roman philosophy in the first two centuries of the Common Era. Hence we are now ready to study *ancient* neo-Aristotelianism in a disciplined and philosophically alert way. This is what "ethics after Aristotle" means— ethics after the model of and in the manner of Aristotle, and ethics in the half millennium after his death.

At this point we need to review quickly the key players who will appear as ancient neo-Aristotelians in these pages.[21] The first and most familiar is Theophrastus, the collaborator of Aristotle who was also the founder of the institution dedicated to his intellectual legacy, the Lyceum. His contributions to moral theory went well beyond mere tinkering with details and elaboration. Next comes a shadowy figure who may well have been a contemporary of Theophrastus, a student or follower, but whose name is forever lost to us (though since he appears frequently in the next chapter I'll have to baptize him temporarily). He is anonymous because his work, a treatise in ethics drawing selectively and critically (and not always competently or intelligently) on both the *Nicomachean* and *Eudemian Ethics,* was attributed to Aristotle himself. That the treatise we know as the *Magna Moralia* (*MM*) even survived at all is a result of this misattribution,[22] for it is certainly not a treatise of high philosophical quality. Still, it shows signs of being the work of someone with an independent and distinct approach (including a certain openness towards Plato, which was shared by some other Peripatetics as well, such as Clearchus and Heraclides), and we will do the author more justice if we approach him in that spirit.

Neo-Aristotelian ideas about ethics also emerge from a reading of the fragments of that great natural philosopher, Strato of Lampsacus. Known best for his independent theorizing in physics, he was more conventional in ethics than his follower Lycon, who in turn was outdone by the innovative Hieronymus of Rhodes, still in the third century BCE.[23] But it is in the second century BCE that things, if you will, break wide open. In chapter 3 I will argue that Critolaus is the unsung hero of our story, a highly creative neo-Aristotelian, responsive to his dialectical environment, who set the agenda for the following 150 years of philosophical work in the Aristotelian mode.[24] We see evidence of his influence in Cicero especially, no doubt through the influence of Antiochus of Ascalon and others in the first century

BCE. Perhaps the peak of neo-Aristotelian thinking before Alexander is visible in book 5 of Cicero's *On Goals*.

The Imperial period brought dramatic social changes that had great impact on intellectual life, and we see evidence of very significant developments in philosophy. Among other developments, we see the rise of textbook philosophy, doxographies and encyclopedias of a kind familiar to students of later antiquity and to those who depend on such sources for the history of earlier centuries. When an unknown Peripatetic sat down to organize what we now call Doxography C,[25] he assembled a document testifying to innovation driven by competition with Stoic and Platonic thinking. In the same period, we see evidence of an increased Aristotelian engagement with the topic of the passions—a theme on which any Aristotelian worth his salt would thereafter have to take a stand. And when Aristotelians did so, Stoics were ready to push back with arguments supporting their own position on the issue. In fact, the latter half of the first century CE provides abundant evidence of vigorous ethical debate between Aristotelians and Stoics, with important implications for both schools.

When we come to the outburst of intellectual creativity in the second century CE, Aristotelian ethics has been, in a way, transformed. In the second century Aristotelians reengage with Platonism, both schools now renewing themselves by the route, perhaps implausible to us, of the commentary tradition and works written for school use. Platonists, such as Plutarch, Alcinous, and Atticus, drew freely on Aristotelians, who in turn revitalized their own theories by reconnecting more directly and in a new, less independent-minded spirit with Aristotle's own works. It is no accident that we now find the first surviving commentary on Aristotle's ethics (that by Aspasius).[26] The climax of ancient neo-Aristotelianism in ethics, though, is Alexander of Aphrodisias, the greatest Peripatetic since Aristotle and without a doubt the most influential ancient voice in the reshaping of Aristotelian ethics. His treatise *On Fate* touched on ethics in several important ways;[27] but for our purposes the focus will be on some of Alexander's lesser-known essays on ethics, which take on Stoic opposition, Platonist recalcitrance, and the inevitable obscurities of the master himself. In these essays the spirit is exegetical, systematizing, reverential, and yet open to change. It is with Alexander that I will end my selective exploration of ancient neo-Aristotelianism in ethics; it never did get any better than that. All that remained, in the ancient world at least, was for Platonists to exploit the refashioned works of Plato's greatest student to their own ends.

Five hundred years of debate and doctrinal development will reveal a lot of variety. And yet it will all be Aristotelian. My hope is that at the end of this inevitably sketchy treatment of the tradition we might be able to identify some key features of Aristotelian ethics and then return, all too briefly, to think again about the problem about today with which we began.

Later Aristotelians innovated for a variety of reasons: the need to engage with contemporary debate, the desire to sort out what look like gaps or confusions in the works of Aristotle himself, and philosophical disagreement with the master and each other. Let me begin with a quick and selective survey of some of the loose ends left by Aristotle, beyond the larger concern about naturalism and ethical method already mentioned. I will try to say a bit about each of these in the pages that follow, but I won't linger unduly over these issues, as the problems are, at least in outline, familiar to students of Aristotle.

One of the most obvious issues is the nature of pleasure and its relationship to happiness. It is an issue not least because Aristotle's works on ethics contain two similar but (in my view) ultimately incompatible analyses of pleasure, one in *Eudemian Ethics* 6 (a book which also appears in our corpus as *Nicomachean Ethics* 7) and the other in *Nicomachean Ethics* 10. As G. E. L. Owen summed it up,[28]

> What [the *Eudemian Ethics* account] says and [the *Nicomachean Ethics* account] appears to deny, is that pleasures are just the unhindered activities of our natural faculties. In both contexts the activities are such basic ingredients of a man's life as the exercises of his intelligence. By identifying pleasures with such activities [the *Eudemian Ethics*] can argue that the best life for man may simply be some pleasure or class of pleasures (1153b7–13). By distinguishing them [the *Nicomachean Ethics*] can leave it an open question whether we choose the life for the sake of pleasure or *vice versa* (1175a18–21).

Debate on the issue has not ceased since Owen wrote, but even this brief description shows what is at stake. On one view, Aristotle might even be regarded as some sort of hedonist, for the key elements of the *telos* are pleasures (whatever else they might also be).[29] On the other view, he can deny being a hedonist without having to concede to Speusippus's antipleasure agenda in ethics (something which even Plato balked at in the last analysis, if we are to judge by his late dialogue *Philebus*). Finding a significant, positive role for pleasure, at least as *part* of the motivational story for human beings, helps Aristotle to give his normative theory a generality that it would otherwise lack. The question of naturalism comes up again and again in the history of ancient ethics, a question about whether the fundamentals of ethics are part of a general or even universal theory that also operates in other parts of the natural world. Though Aristotle rejects Eudoxus's explicit argument that pleasure is the good *because* it is the goal for all animal species, a position that later Aristotelians met in its Epicurean version, he did appreciate the explanatory power of naturalism in this sense—as he did when defining happiness as the perfect fulfillment of species-relative natural capacities.

We see this in book I of his *Nicomachean Ethics*, in chapter 7.[30] This is where we find the so-called function argument which purports to show that the *telos* for man is identifiable as a set of activities in accordance with the excellent condition of the distinctive traits of our species. Put this way, our "goal" is fully generalizable and the same formulation works throughout the natural world (and among the tools used by the crafts, as well), or at least in that subset of it which is governed by the teleology and functionalism found most prominently in Aristotle's biology—a scientific insight into the entire natural world which also becomes a basic principle of Aristotle's metaphysics. To the extent that the function argument captures the core insights of Aristotle's theory it is a strongly naturalistic theory of normativity and moral motivation. The issue of naturalism in this sense is never without controversy. For as Julia Annas's critique of the function argument[31] shows—and as studies of the detailed theory of specifically Aristotelian virtues suggest[32]—there is a tension between this kind of teleological theory of ethics (which leaves human beings no different in relation to their specific nature than other animals are with respect to theirs) and the intuition—implied in the opinions of the many and the wise, the *endoxa*—that we human beings are special. This preference for seeing ourselves as special comes out in two ways: the detailed account of particular virtues depends on the particular social practices of a given society and on the views of the many and the wise; and the specialness that humans possess seems at times to break away from merely human nature. When Aristotle claims, following a Greek tradition that prominently includes Plato, that the important thing about human aspirations is to strive for the divine, to step outside our nature, to look above merely human nature for our ultimate values, then that (like the reliance on the contingent facts of a particular Greek social order and its conventions) seems to constitute a limitation on the species-oriented, functional principles of biological naturalism. We see these principles in the argument that identifies our *telos* as excellent activity in accordance with the distinctive capacities of our species; a problem arises when Aristotle's conception of human perfection crosses over from the distinctively human nature to embrace the divine as well—how will this be part of his naturalistic theory, especially given that god, unlike humans, is not part of nature? God has no capacities to actualize—he is pure activity. He is not a part of the contingent world of change; as animals with a nature, we are. He has no internal principle of motion and rest, since he neither moves nor rests in the way that natural things do. The very idea that human thriving (that is, actualizing distinctive human potentials) should also require an activity not grounded in a potentiality or capacity is, to say the least, a challenge. This tension over naturalism is built in to Aristotle's ethics, and ethics after Aristotle remains seized with the problem.

Another loose end in the ethics concerns the role of luck, the contingencies of ordinary human lives, and the availability of noncharacter goods (whether those of the body or the goods that are external to a human being but nevertheless of great importance for his or her life). Are luck and the external goods which largely depend on it, even bodily goods, necessary for a happy life? Our happiness consists (in part or as a whole) in activities that accord with distinctively human excellences, excellences of the rational soul. These activities can be undermined or even blocked by factors beyond our control such as poverty, poor health, accidents of birth, and the grand strokes of fate sometimes called Priamic misfortunes.[33] Aristotle concedes that such things have a significant impact, but the degree to which and the way in which they do so is unclear. Aristotle was conflicted, not unreasonably, and in my view it would be a brave or willful interpreter who claimed to know Aristotle's final view.

The same holds for another familiar point of contention, the relationship between the contemplative or purely intellectual virtues (and their activities) and the activities and applications of practical intellect. In an excellent human life, which should be dominant? Is intellectual excellence just one among many excellences or does it tower decisively over the others? Can a person be truly happy in the absence of what we would call a significant life of the mind? If one is lucky enough and wise enough to be living the life of contemplative excellence, are the moral excellences nevertheless essential to one's happiness? Are they merely means to that end? Or is action in accordance with moral excellence also indispensable to a successful life?

More subtle than this is a worry about the role of passions in a good human life. That virtues are "mean" states is clear—among nonspecialists this is perhaps Aristotle's best-known doctrine. But what about the passions? They aren't dispositions—as virtues are. So we cannot assume that they are all meant to be states of moderation as well. Aristotle hints, of course, that moderation in *all* things is good for human life, but does he apply this to all the passions? Is rage to be moderated? Lust? Shyness? Pride? What would the mean state of that *pathos* be in, say, the great-souled man? Aristotle leaves many loose ends in his treatment of the passions, including (as we see in his subtle though puzzling account of *akrasia*) the relationship between the *pathē* and *logos*. The binary contrast, "reason vs. passion," does not achieve a sharp definition in Aristotle himself, not even as sharp a definition as it had in Plato. But it certainly emerges in his school after him.

Finally, anyone who read both versions of Aristotle's *Ethics* would naturally be puzzled, if not disturbed, by one of the most salient differences between them. The attentive reader notices quickly that it is a distinctive feature of the *Nicomachean* version that it emphatically places the study of social and political life, *politikē*, at the top of the hierarchy of sciences. The study of ethics is subordinated to it both at the beginning and at the end of the work. Not so in the *Eudemian* version—though less decisive about such matters than in the *Nicomachean*, in the *Eudemian Ethics* Aristotle seems ready to grant to ethics itself a superordinate status, or at the least to play an equal role with political science in determining what is most vital for the good human life.[34] The problem is an old one; in fact, it is also a Platonic worry: in *Republic* book 7 Socrates concedes that the guardians may not be happiest if they give up philosophy for a period of years to administer the ideal state, Kallipolis, but holds nevertheless that the imperatives of the city require it of them. It is only their well-developed sense of justice that protects them from lingering discontent over the sacrifice. But it *is* a sacrifice. Socrates displays, I think, mixed feelings on the issue throughout the dialogue. And Aristotle also seems to have wobbled. So we will not be shocked to find his successors struggling with it too.

These are not trivial issues—not even the worry about the passions.[35] Schools could split over hedonism;[36] it would not have been unreasonable to reject a teacher who put politics ahead of ethics or to expel a student who came to believe that happiness is vulnerable to luck or that those without a gift for contemplation and a good supply of coarse external goods could never be happy. In the ancient world of eudaimonism these are, or can be, decisive points of disagreement. Yet the neo-Aristotelians of the Hellenistic world did disagree on all these points and still they clung together. It will take the rest of this book to discover what, in anything, kept the school together in the face of this variety.

In the chapters which follow I will pursue these themes as we find them in what survives of the ethical works of Aristotelians in the Hellenistic and early Imperial periods. But as I have indicated, the process of reacting to Aristotle's often nuanced ethical theory began in his own lifetime, with the work of his student and collaborator Theophrastus. So it is perhaps appropriate to conclude this introductory chapter with a quick look at his contributions. Theophrastus is best known as the author of the *Characters*,[37] and he wrote on a wide range of ethical topics. His *Ethics* (or *Ethical Lectures* or *On Character States—ēthē*)[38] apparently covered themes also listed as separate works: the passions, the voluntary, virtue and its varieties, several particular virtues, happiness, good fortune, child-rearing, punishment, friendship, *charis* (gratitude), pleasure and false pleasure, social interaction.[39] There were distinct works on grief (the *Callisthenes*),[40] ways of life *(peri biōn)*,[41] on marriage[42] (possibly part of *peri biōn*, as may also be the case for *On Old Age, On Wealth, On Ambition, On Flattery, On Erōs,* and *On Drunkenness*[43]). Like Aristotle, he wrote a *Protreptic.*[44]

Since most of this work is fragmentary or known only through second-hand reports, it is usually impossible to tell whether or how Theophrastus changed or challenged Aristotle's views. But there was clearly no reluctance to innovate and the record indicates significant changes in connection with the *pathē*,[45] with the roles of the practical and the theoretical in the good life,[46] and with the interdependent issues of external goods and the vulnerability of virtue to chance.[47] He may also have taken further even than Aristotle did in *Nicomachean Ethics* I.13 the tendency to treat ethical matters outside the constraints of his "scientific" hylomorphic analysis of the soul and body. Aristotle acknowledges that the political theorist and moral philosopher need not have the most precise grasp available of the nature of the soul and its relationship to the body and then goes on adopt an analysis of the soul's powers which he attributes to unspecified exoteric works (1102a26–27), perhaps his own youthful *Protreptic*; this turns out to resemble closely views found in Plato's *Republic* and *Timaeus*; in fact, all of Aristotle's discussions of weak and strong will (*akrasia* and *enkrateia*) rely on this framework[48] and its relationship to the hylomorphic analysis of soul and the division of soul into hierarchically organized capacities (growth and reproduction, perception, thought, etc.) is never fully clarified. This is one of the issues on which Aristotle overtly raises a question about the connection between a scientific, naturalistic theory about human ethics to views based on the *endoxa* (as reflected also in the "exoteric" works).

Theophrastus takes this tendency to bracket out moral psychology from "scientific" psychology one step further. In discussing failures to control desire and passion he clearly adopts the broadly Platonic model that Aristotle employed (see 441 = Marcus Aurelius 2.10), but his embrace of the language of body/soul dualism in a similar context goes far beyond anything we find in Aristotle's ethical treatises. In a striking bit of evidence (440A), the author of *On Desire and Grief* (an anonymous work preserved in the corpus of Plutarch) compares Theophrastus with Democritus, who also used dualistic language about body and soul:

> Theophrastus . . . said that the soul inhabits the body at great cost. For a brief period it pays heavy fees: feelings of grief, fright, desire, jealousy. Since it encounters these feelings in the body, the soul might more justly bring suit against the body for mutilation, with regard to the things it has forgotten, and for acts of violence, with regard to the way in which it is held down, and for *hubris*, with regard to things it suffers through contempt and abuse, being blamed quite unfairly for the evils of the body.[49]

This dualistic vision reminds us of the *Phaedo* with its attribution of the *pathē* to the body and the assumption that *logos* is the main feature of the soul; it scarcely seems Peripatetic in spirit,[50] but it was certainly Theophrastan. Porphyry reports the same view (440C = *On Abstinence* 4.20), and the genuine Plutarch does so as well (440B = *De tuenda sanitate* 135d–e); like Porphyry, Plutarch quotes Theophrastus's technical term for the price soul pays to the body—it is a rental fee *(enoikion)*, suggestive of a relationship between two more or less autonomous actors—but acknowledging that it is a metaphor. Perhaps Theophrastus's adoption of a body/soul dualism occurred in some popular work, such as his *Protreptic*, though no source says so.[51] He would no doubt have conceded, like Aristotle, that there is another, more scientific way to look at such matters. But flirtation with such starkly dualistic views is one thing in the young Aristotle (*if* he was young and Platonizing when he wrote his *Protreptic*) and quite another in the mature work of his successor and head of the school.

On the nature and role of the passions Theophrastus was relatively conservative, though his views on anger have a surprising prominence in the surviving evidence.[52] Theophrastus was equally conservative on the notion of the mean. Although 449A (= Stobaeus 2.7, pp. 140–142 Wachsmuth) suggests that some *pathē* should be moderated if the associated dispositions are to be good, this is still not the explicit doctrine of *metriopatheia* which (according to an unpublished paper by Emily Fletcher) arguably appears first in the *Magna Moralia*.[53] A more striking case of Theophrastan connection to the *Magna Moralia* arises with the complicated question of how practical and theoretical wisdom are related. Aristotle, as we have seen, had a complicated position. Theophrastus had a much more straightforward view:[54]

Theophrastus, at least, says that practical wisdom is related to theoretical wisdom in a way similar to the way in which slaves acting
as stewards of their masters are related to their masters. For they
do everything which must be done within the house, in order that
their masters may have leisure for the pursuits appropriate to free
men. And practical wisdom arranges what must be done, in order that
theoretical wisdom may have leisure for the contemplation of things
most valuable.

The *Magna Moralia* seems to echo this Theophrastan view, even picking
up the image of the house-steward (I.34.31). What Theophrastus
says here seems to be a rather extreme version of what Aristotle says
in the final paragraphs of *Eudemian Ethics* 8, but in taking such a firm,
instrumentalist line on the question Theophrastus embraces a view
which it is hard to accept as straightforwardly Aristotelian. The ten-
sions and hesitations of the master are resolved by adopting a position
which is clearer, cleaner, and that much less subtle; a position which
is, to some readers, less attractive precisely because it shows how far
Aristotelians were willing to go in instrumentalizing moral virtue for
the sake of individual intellectual achievement.

This tendency to make decisive but somewhat crude determina-
tions where Aristotle himself is more hesitant, may in fact have been
a characteristic feature of Theophrastus's ethics. On the question of
whether misfortune, bad luck, and deficiency in external or bodily
goods could undermine an otherwise happy life, it is difficult to pin
down Aristotle's final view. In a sense, we can see what his view *ought* to
have been—in my view, anyway, it should be something rather like the
eventual Stoic position—much as that would strain against the natural and naturalistic view that health and modest material comfort are

necessary components of the good (or at least, of the best) life. But Aristotle's dominant position on the matter, that happiness is an activity in accordance with excellence of the rational aspect of soul, doesn't leave a clear intrinsic role for these natural goods; and on a reasonable, if somewhat austere, interpretation of Aristotle's eudaimonism, happiness should persist even as we use that rationality to cope with bankruptcy, cancer, or the deaths of loved ones. It should fail only when reason itself fails, which for a hylomorphist or physicalist will occur when a distinct subset of our physical organs fails. The rest of the body should be reason's raw material, not its external equipment (*ektos chorēgia*).[55] But Aristotle clearly can't bring himself to adopt this view cleanly and the tension in both of his *Ethics* has provided fodder for discussion and debate ever since.

Theophrastus[56] seems to have cut the Gordian knot in his *On Happiness*.[57] Cicero tells us (493 = *TD* 5.24–5) that Theophrastus was wonderfully consistent on the question—external and bodily misfortunes *can* ruin happiness. And he said something just as outrageous (in Cicero's view) in his *Callisthenes*: fortune, not wisdom, is *in charge of life*. Perhaps this last remark was in a consolatory context, but its import is clear. Fortune can be fought off to some extent through cultivation of the virtues (as reported by Vitruvius in fr. 491 = *De architectura* 6), but in the final analysis, if things we cannot decisively control—such as our financial and physical conditions—are actually *bad*, then our happiness is not up to us. It is only fair to observe that most of the evidence for this view comes from Cicero, whose views are sometimes excessively shaped by contemporary Greek philosophers who may not have been dispassionate on the issues (492–500);[58] but none of it rings false. Aristotle left a genuine problem; Theophrastus resolved the issue by taking a position that would have been too starkly consistent for his master.[59]

It should be no surprise that Theophrastus was so ready to dis-agree with his colleague and friend, the older genius in whose wake he had for many years been pushing back frontiers in meteorology, botany, and in many other areas of enquiry. Theophrastus's inde-pendence of mind also became clear in his *Metaphysics*,[60] a work in which he had no compunction about challenging some of Aristotle's boldest theories, not least the claim that the cosmos is moved by an unmoved mover, a god who stands outside nature.[61] His independent line on the nature of the *telos* and the conditions for human happiness was certainly no more radical than that—and that such challenges could emerge from Aristotle's closest intellectual associate tells us as much, I think, as we need to know about the latitude inherent in Aris-totelianism. When we turn, in the next chapter, to consider the next phase of Aristotelian ethics in the ancient world, it will be important to keep this latitude in mind.

2

Flirting with Hedonism
(It's Only Natural)

In chapter I, I suggested that the *Magna Moralia* (*MM*) sometimes pushes Aristotelian innovation even further than Theophrastus does. Reading the *MM* is a constant process of noting the various ways in which the author either responds to problems and uncertainties in Aristotle or adapts in reaction to contemporary developments. The author is unknown, and so I propose to call him "Magnus," adopting the name from some wag at a highly productive workshop on the *Magna Moralia* at Cambridge University in 2010. Referring to the author as "anonymous" or "pseudo-Aristotle" or (even worse) as "the author of the *Magna Moralia*" is a somewhat alienating practice; it is markedly more difficult to think about the philosophical intent and character of the text with that sort of stigma attached. A specific nom-de-plume works better, at least for me.

Magnus, then, aims to present a version of Aristotelian ethics which draws on both the *Nicomachean* and the *Eudemian* books. And often he seems to strike out on his own, as when he declares (2.10.6-7

= 1208a31–b2) that his treatise is aimed *not* at making people happy (by teaching the use and application of the theory) but only at presenting the theory itself. imparting what seems to be a cognitive disposition, like any other branch of knowledge (*epistēmē*). This is in contrast with Aristotle's own position (*NE* 2.2.1 (1103b26–31).): "the present enquiry is *not* for the sake of theory, like others, but for the sake of making us good, since otherwise it would be useless." No doubt Magnus is sometimes just confused or dull, but it is obvious to most readers that he is not always just being inaccurate or clumsy in his presentation of what he finds in Aristotle. Sometimes he really does have his own view, Aristotelian in the broad sense, but not Aristotle's; and this is what he presents, though sometimes awkwardly. We have seen in chapter 1 that Magnus exploits Aristotle's notion of the mean only in connection with the passions (rather than actions *and* passions) and he claims that virtues *just are* mean states of the *pathē* (*MM* I.22.1 = 1191b25–29). Whether this is exactly the doctrine of *metriopatheia* later attributed to Aristotelian theory is not completely clear.[1] But it is certainly an innovation and it makes a narrower claim than does Aristotle's theory that the virtues are states which aim at means in actions as well as passions; it also goes well with this author's general tendency to see human nature in terms of a fundamental dualism of reason and passion (*logos* and *pathos*)[2] and, I would suggest, with a set of philosophical worries and debates about the nature of the passions initiated by Stoics in the early Hellenistic period.

Further evidence of our author's independence of mind lies in the long recognized fact that he has little interest in the role of contemplation in the happy life. In fact, as the author sets out his version of Aristotelian doctrine about purely theoretical wisdom, he feels compelled to defend its very inclusion in a work on ethics, which in his view is fundamentally a political treatise (1.34.21–22 = 1197b28–35). The figure of Anaxagoras never appears as a hero of theoretical philosophy, as happens several times in Aristotle.[3] There is a frank emphasis on the practical nature of moral philosophy: it is *phronēsis* not *sophia* which is the architect of the virtues (1.34.29 = 1198b4–8) and the nonpractical intellectual virtues seem to be present in the treatise on sufferance, not as a key part (indeed the most important part) of the good life for human beings.

For all that, Magnus (like Theophrastus at times) is also noticeably sympathetic to several Platonic doctrines. For example, the form of the good is only rejected as being irrelevant to practical philosophy, not rejected without qualification (*MM* 1.1.8 = 1182a26–30). Moreover, Magnus is surprisingly negative about distinctively Socratic views. Aristotle's own assessment of Socrates is subtle and often appreciative. Magnus, however, only mentions Socrates to criticize him, mostly for his alleged "intellectualism."[4]

A host of small differences could be listed, not always readily systemizable. Magnus is exceptionally emphatic—more even than Aristotle himself—about the importance of using *archai* and methods which are narrowly pertinent to the subject matter. He offers us a different etymology for the key term *prohairesis* (1.17.3–4 = 1189a13–16), opting for the preferential sense of *pro* (glossed with *anti*), rather than the temporal sense of the *Nicomachean Ethics* (3.2 = 1112a15–17) and is subtly more inclined to consequentialist-sounding features in his analysis of choice (1.17.9 = 1189b16–17): "based on the outcomes, whichever seem to be better, we choose these things and do so *for this reason.*" He will cheerfully use *kinēsis* and *energeia* as synonyms when discussing pleasure (2.7) and seems strikingly open to the hedonist side of Aristotle's hesitations on the role of pleasure in happiness. Magnus takes an original (if unsophisticated) position on the question of the sources of moral error (1.18.2 = 1190a5-7).

In his view it is fundamentally pleasure and pain that distort our reasoning processes; simple errors in reasoning matter less. Again, this is unsurprising in an author who tends to emphasize the polar opposition of *logos* to *pathos* and shows little interest in the subtleties of Aristotle's views on practical reason in its relationship to desire. Magnus puts a systematically greater emphasis on the influence of the passions on our choices than Aristotle did and focusses less sharply on the strictly cognitive aspects of our decision processes—not surprising, one might well think, in a philosopher who says that the virtues just are moderate states of the *pathē*. As Magnus says (2.3.17 = 1200a30–32):[5] "in general, since at the outset we specified that the virtues are mean states [*mesotētes*] it is also the case that what is more of a virtue is more of a mean."

Still on the topic of pleasure and pain, Magnus takes a fresh approach to the importance to happiness of pleasure and the absence of pain (2.7), anticipating[6] the views of the Peripatetic Hieronymus when he claims that "every pleasure is a good." For example (2.7.13– 16 = 1205a26–b13), in response to the charge that some pleasures are base (*phaulon*) and so that pleasure as such cannot be a good, he argues that the same would apply to knowledge—some knowledge is base as well, and yet we do not deny that knowledge as such is a good. Correspondingly, some parts of nature are (as Aristotle himself noted, even while agreeing that this was no reason not to study them) pretty revolting and base,[7] yet we do not on that account treat nature *itself* as base—a point that Aristotle would heartily endorse but which he never brought to bear on *this* question. Indeed, base pleasures, Magnus suggests, are those of base natures, such as those of brute beasts; if a nature is fine (*kalon*), as human nature is, then its pleasures will also be fine. He singles out the pleasures which restore our nature to its proper state—and so they are good to just that extent.

Magnus is also more attentive to the role of natural inclinations in our moral life,[8] going so far as to claim (2.7.30–31 = 1206b17–29) that reason is not the basic starting point or *archē* for virtue:

> In general it is not the case, as others think, that reason is the starting point and leading factor in virtue, but rather the passions are. For there must first be in us an *irrational inclination* towards the fine [*kalon*]—and there actually is such a thing—and then subsequently reason must cast its ballot in favor of it and make the final decision. And one might see this by observing children and those who live without reason. For in them there first arise, *without reason, inclinations* of the passions towards the fine, and later on reason comes along and by voting in favor makes them do what is fine. But it isn't the case that the passions will agree and follow along if one starts out towards what is fine on the basis of reason; usually the passions resist. That is why the passionate element in us, when it is in good condition, is more like a starting point for virtue than reason is.

This is a significant difference of emphasis on the relative roles of reason and the passionate inclinations from what we find in Aristotle. Our author, awkward as he may be at times, has a mind of his own and is committed to some distinctive philosophical positions differing from Aristotle's at least in nuance. Further, in his second book (at 2.8.1) he follows up on the Theophrastan recognition of external goods and treats them clearly as necessary conditions for happiness: "For without external goods, over which fortune is authoritative, it is not possible to be happy" (1206b33–34).[9] Since he also recognizes the importance to virtue of our ability to control circumstances (having key factors in our own power, *eph' hēmin*, is necessary for being virtuous), it will follow that unfortunate people simply will not be able to achieve happiness. A careful analysis of Aristotle's own exploration of this question yields less than crisp results, and sympathetic readers can come to different conclusions. But my own inclination is to focus first and foremost on passages like the following from the *Nicomachean Ethics:*

> Given that many things happen by chance, things that differ in magnitude and smallness, small instances of good fortune, and similarly of the opposite, clearly do not alter the balance of a man's life, whereas turns of fortune that are great and repeated will if good make one's life more blessed (since they are themselves such as to add lustre to life, and the use of them is fine and worthwhile), and if they turn out in the opposite way, they crush and maim one's blessedness; for they bring on pains, and obstruct many sorts of activities. Nevertheless, even in these circumstances the quality of fineness shines through, when someone bears repeated and great misfortunes calmly, not because he is insensitive to them but because he is a person of nobility and greatness of soul. If one's activities are what determine the quality of one's life, as we have said, no one who is blessed will become miserable; for he will never do what is hateful and vile. For we consider that the truly good and sensible person bears what fortune brings him with good grace, and acts on each occasion in the finest way given the resources at the time, just as we think that a good general uses the army he has to the best strategic advantage, and a shoemaker makes a shoe as finely as it can be made out of the hides he has been given; and similarly with all other sorts of craftsmen. If so, then the happy man will never become miserable, though neither will he be blessed if he meets with fortunes like Priam's. (*NE* 1100b22–1101a8, tr. Rowe.)

In the *Eudemian Ethics* Aristotle resists making genuine happiness depend on good fortune, even while acknowledging (in 8.2) that there are people who lack genuine virtue but nevertheless "do well" (that is, enjoy *eupragia*) in life. In this same chapter of the *Eudemian Ethics* Aristotle comes close (at 1247b18–28) to making the point that Magnus makes—in fact, on this topic the *Magna Moralia* is pretty clearly following the *Eudemian* more closely than the *Nicomachean Ethics*—that one can have irrationally based inclinations for the good which lead to getting things right *(katorthoun)* on a consistent basis, even without the virtues of the rational part of the soul playing a role. It is only reasonable to acknowledge the existence of this kind of contingency, but Aristotle cannot bring himself to make virtue or happiness *dependent* on it, while Magnus evidently does not feel so constrained; hence he leaves considerably more room for plain dumb luck and the impersonal chance of natural processes to affect *happiness* and the excellent states of character on which it depends.

When Cicero mentions this aspect of Theophrastus's ethical thought he dismisses it as a sign of weakness,[10] and it is easy to imagine how he would have reacted to the even more extreme position taken in the *Magna Moralia*. But one may wonder if that assessment is really fair to these two early neo-Aristotelians. True enough, it can seem like a "weak" or "soft" position when it is set beside the Stoic insistence (which Cicero also at times finds extreme) that virtue is *completely* in our control and that it suffices for happiness, no matter what happens to us in our physical and social lives. The Stoic doctrine is certainly high-minded, and it is, moreover, one that follows logically from a rigorous interpretation of the view that happiness just is a sustained pattern of activity in accordance with stable rational excellences. But recognition of the contingency of life, of the unfairness of unequal opportunities, of the fact that those who don't do well in the lottery that governs social origins and genetic inheritance—factors that seem to us moderns to have such power over our well-being—also seems to be the result of honest and direct observation of the human condition. Theophrastus and Magnus at times simply seem to be more consistently

36

realistic than Aristotle was. The master sets the bar for happiness very high; he urges us to be most human in becoming godlike, and he struggles with the need to acknowledge that sometimes virtue is not enough for happiness. What we see here, I think, is a struggle within Aristotelian ethics over the conditions of happiness, a hesitancy between the highest aspirations we can have for human reason and the sometimes deflationary view, rooted in more careful and naturalistic observation of human affairs, of how human beings actually live.

Though a great deal more could be said about the version of Aristotelianism found in the *Magna Moralia*, I would like now to shift from Magnus to a rather more challenging set of neo-Aristotelians, philosophers whose names and approximate dates we do know but whose views are only spottily preserved. The usual story about Aristotle's school in the Hellenistic period is one of steep decline and stagnation—an exaggeration, in my view, but not fundamentally wrong. The most important developments, certainly in ethics, in fact occurred elsewhere, with the rapid growth and development of two major schools, Stoic and Epicurean. Both new schools emphasized the critical role of nature as a reference point for ethics even more than Aristotelians tended to do. Aristotelian developments are harder to document (only the *Magna Moralia* is preserved more or less intact from the period) and within the school it seems clear that the main focus was on natural philosophy; this is certainly what Strato of Lampsacus is best known for and Theophrastus himself was prolific in physics. That, of course, surely tended to increase the pressure on Aristotelian ethics to emphasize its naturalistic side—not only did Stoics argue that following nature (in their own way) is the key to ethics, and the Epicureans argue that our material nature is the foundation of our happiness in pleasure, but within the Aristotelian school itself natural philosophy was in the driver's seat. We should not be surprised, then,

37

that a kind of naturalism came to the fore in their ethics, as I think we can see that it did.[11]

Regrettably, the ethical work of Strato of Lampsacus (the next head of the school after Theophrastus) is less well documented than his physics and certainly less important to later tradition. But as Stephen White noted some years ago,[12] Strato's many ethical works did include one striking definition that fortunately still survives: the good is "what perfects the capacity/potential [*dunamis*] through which we achieve activity/actuality [*energeia*]."[13] This is certainly not Aristotle's definition of the good, though it is significant that Strato generates a definition of the good that depends on concepts drawn from Aristotle's scientific and metaphysical theories. Happiness is an activity in accordance with certain rational excellences, the best actualization of characteristically human capacities. The inclination to produce a single, univocal definition of the good is not in the spirit of Aristotle's ethics, but it is not difficult to imagine the context which would encourage this move. Is it Aristotelian in a way other than by employing some bits of his metaphysical theory? Would Aristotle, who in a loose sort of way recognizes three kinds of good (those of the soul, those of the body, and external goods),[14] want to limit goods to those assets which perfectly enhance our ability to be happy? Is this "that at which everything aims" and the goal of all organized intellectual activities, as Aristotle claims in the opening lines of the *Nicomachean Ethics?* Is happiness itself, the activity which goods make possible, not a good? Do the gods not enjoy goods? That would be a view more radical even than that of our friend Magnus in the *Magna Moralia*, who was emphatic in claiming that human good was fundamentally different from divine good (I.I, 1182b3–4).

So perhaps Strato was really only talking about human goods. It is possible that Strato is just being misreported here, but it is more likely,

I think, that (as White suggested) Strato is primarily focused on a particular problem, that is, the difficult question of how one becomes virtuous. But if that is so, then this evidence reveals that he has a particular and very practical interest in just one part of Aristotle's ethical enquiry, moral education. How do I become virtuous? What do I need to get my capacities and dispositions in ideal working order? These are the practical questions we might naturally turn to once the goal of ethical enquiry has been settled.[15] Does Strato's Aristotelianism in ethics consist in this focus on practical ways and means, to the exclusion of debate about the larger issues? If so, it stands in stark contrast to the overtly theoretical aim of Magnus's treatise.

Lycon, from northwestern Anatolia, headed the school after Strato,[16] perhaps around 269 BCE, and may well have remained head for over forty years, until his death around 225,[17] an astonishingly long period of intellectual leadership. Known to the tradition as an eloquent, witty speaker, a sharp dresser, and a generous, perhaps even lavish, host,[18] he, in part through his political connections and personal wealth, helped the school to thrive despite his reputation for being an intellectual lightweight.[19] Despite this caricature, familiar to us from the kind of intermittent and snide carping about successful administrators which sometimes blights university life, Lycon is known to have taken strong views in ethics, the most important of which was his definition of the *telos* (i.e., *eudaimonia*) as "true joy [*chara*] of the soul . . .[20] at fine things [*epi tois kalois*]." Despite Stephen White's ingenuity,[21] it does not seem plausible to me that this redefinition of happiness was a dialectical move against the Stoics. More likely is the thought that Lycon was in favor of a more hedonistic interpretation of Aristotelian ethics than (say) Antiochus or Cicero in a later time would have felt comfortable with. But Aristotle's own works contain the seeds of this openness to the role played by pleasure in the happy life.

If the "fine things" in question are fine actions, then to say that the goal is a genuine pleasure attendant on those actions would be to offer an Aristotelian account of the goal that grants somewhat greater weight to such satisfactions than either of Aristotle's own accounts did. The *Eudemian Ethics* shares the *Nicomachean* view that happiness is an optimal activity, but holds also that pleasure itself *is* an unimpeded activity of a natural capacity (rather than being something which accompanies or supervenes on such activities). In both *Ethics* Aristotle is clear that the good life ought to be characterized by pleasures, and Lycon's formulation of the *telos* has elements in common with both versions, though it has clearly developed beyond Aristotle's theory by finding a more prominent place for pleasure in the best life—perhaps even beyond what we see in the *Magna Moralia*. The drive to be active in accordance with our proper capacities just is, on this view, a drive for pleasure of a particularly refined kind. So the charge of hedonism against Lycon is not unreasonable.[22] Whether this kind of hedonism is actually un-Aristotelian in any important sense is a quite different question.

This hedonism is not, however, based on the kinds of considerations advanced in the fourth century by Aristotle's associate and friend Eudoxus, who had essentially argued for hedonism on the basis of the alleged fact that all animals pursue pleasure—that it is a universal and so natural feature of animal life. This argument had been rejected by Aristotle in *Nicomachean Ethics* book 10; in the *Nicomachean Ethics* pleasure is not constitutive of the activity which is happiness, but reliably accompanies it. What motivates us is the drive to activity in accordance with our characteristic rational excellence. Are we, though, different from the rest of the natural world in being so motivated? Aristotle's way of approaching the issue emphasizes what distinguishes humans from other animals, and even focusses on what makes us like the gods. Despite his interest in natural philosophy and his apparent inclination to make nature something of a reference point for human norms, Aristotle's treatment of the *telos* is sometimes skittish about the relationship of human beings to the rest of nature. But if we are going to treat humans as part of the natural world and not as fallen gods, why would we *not* go looking for an account of moral motivation that places us firmly in the natural world while nevertheless pointing to what makes us special?

Lycon's formulation, I suggest, does just this, and at the same time it preserves features of both Aristotelian versions of the relationship between pleasure and happiness: there is a pleasure attendant on *ta kala* (which may well be the very virtuous actions Aristotle has in mind) and this pleasure just is the goal. It is open to him to say that all animals are motivated by pleasure (as Eudoxus said and as Epicureans emphasized) and that humans share that motivation; our distinguishing feature is simply *what we take pleasure in*, fine or noble deeds, deeds of virtue. If this is right, then Lycon is in fact a hedonist of sorts, but not of the kind which sober moral philosophers need to attack.[23]

Rather than seeing this as nothing but a rejoinder to Stoicism[24] or a concession, perhaps, to Epicurean hedonism, both of which were indeed live forces at the time, it makes just as much sense to interpret this as an attempt to unify Aristotle's two accounts of pleasure and its relationship to happiness. We may easily enough imagine an exegetical context. Agreeing with Aristotle and many others that a conception of *eudaimonia* which omits pleasure would violate our *endoxa*, Lycon tries to resolve an apparent conflict in Aristotle's own theory. And in so doing, he finds a more general basis for Aristotelian ethics, one that emphasizes the situatedness of human beings in the natural world rather than in their relationship to the divine. *Of course* happiness, our greatest motivator, is a kind of pleasure for us, as for all animals, but it can only be a pleasure of the mind directed at or arising from (*epi* could indicate either relationship) just the right kind of actions, actions defined and specified by the moral virtues. Both the *Eudemian* and the *Nicomachean* accounts could be shown to be approximations of the true view, which Lycon's own formula sets out. This would by no means be a surprising form of philosophical interpretation; within the Stoic school Chrysippus seems to have treated at least one of Zeno's own ambiguous formulations in a similar way.[25]

The next version of Aristotelian ethics also involves distinguishing views about pleasure, but Hieronymus[26] seems to have taken a more temperate view than Lycon. Though he may never have headed the school, Hieronymus was a prominent voice in it during Lycon's own headship. According to our biographical evidence (for what it is worth), he somehow provoked the enmity of Lycon (fr. 6 = Diogenes Laërtius 5.67-68) and, despite being a leading opponent of the Academics in the time of Arcesilaus, Hieronymus won the latter's respect.[27] Chrysippus himself thought it worth his while to write a work against Hieronymus, presumably on ethics,[28] in five books (fr. 24 = Philodemus *History of Stoics* PHerc 1018 col.48.1-3). So Hieronymus was not a minor figure in his own lifetime, however obscure he may have become in later centuries.

According to an excellent source,[29] Hieronymus held (fr. 12 = Clement *Strom.* 2.21.127) that the *telos* consists in a life free of disturbance *(to aochlētos zēn)*, but also affirmed the authentically Aristotelian view that only happiness is a *telikon agathon*, the sort of good which *is* an end rather than merely contributing to one. He presumably thought that bodily and external goods were instrumentally valuable, but if he had wanted to include them in the goal then he could also have included in his roster of goods the sort of things which enhance our psychological and moral capacities—as Strato had done.[30] That

Hieronymus did not do so represents a choice within the context of different Aristotelian approaches to ethics.

We might well ask ourselves at this point, as a character in Cicero's *On Goals* did—significantly, it was Marcus Piso—whether someone with Hieronymus's views about the *telos* should be considered a Peripatetic at all (fr. 11 = 5.14).[31] Now Piso, as readers of Cicero know and as we will see for ourselves, is a Peripatetic sympathizer among Academic followers of Antiochus, and his speech contains a great deal of banter about propriety of school membership, sect switching, and philosophical seduction; so there is no reason to take this remark as evidence that Hieronymus's credentials as an Aristotelian were ever seriously challenged in the ancient world—there is no *other* sign that he was doubted and Piso is presumably merely acting in character within the context of the dialogue. Instead, the remark underscores the point that there was room within the big tent of Aristotelian ethics for a fairly wide range of views on central questions.

In assessing the evidence for Hieronymus's version of Aristotelian ethics, a certain caution is called for. Our fullest source for his views (almost the only source besides Clement) is Cicero, and Cicero presents those views in the framework of the *Carneadea divisio* around which he and his teacher organized their understanding of ethics.[32] And in the *ethical* works which mention Hieronymus (the *Tusculan Disputations* as well as the *On Goals*) Cicero usually presents his *telos* as being freedom from *dolor*, pain, whereas in the *Academica* (2.131 = fr. 13A) we find a more accurate rendering of his *telos* (which we know used the term *aochlēsia*), freedom from *molestia*.[33] The position of Hieronymus in Carneades's classification even enabled Cicero to rank him with those who "separated virtue from the goal altogether" (*On Goals* 4.49 = fr. 16C)—which is not even a proper characterization of Epicurus, with whom Hieronymus is here grouped (cf. *On Goals* 5.118 = fr. 22).[34] So we must certainly take account of the apparent distortions produced by this polemical context.

Allowing for the distorting effect of the *Carneadea divisio* (which White attributes rather to Antiochus than to Carneades), we can try to sort out what to make of "a life free of disturbance" as an Aristotelian formulation of the *telos*. I remain unpersuaded by White's attempt to portray Hieronymus, like Lycon, as having "formulate[d] an Aristotelian position in Stoic terms."[35] But I do agree with him[36] that it makes sense to analyze both of their views (Lycon's and Hieronymus's) as critical reactions to Aristotle's position, but reactions from *within* the school. Once we set aside the Carneadean red herring about freedom from *pain*, which Antiochus, Cicero, and others in later antiquity accepted, there is no longer any reason to treat pleasure as the main issue in Hieronymus's conception of the goal of life. Living without disturbance seems a more plausible characterization of his *telos*, and that triggers two strong associations. First,[37] it picks up Aristotle's own preoccupation with the unimpeded character of activity in his formulation of the *telos*. And second, it suggests Epicurus's preoccupation with freedom from disturbance, *tarachē*. Epicurus was far from being the hedonistic whipping boy that Cicero, under the influence of Antiochus and the *Carneadea divisio*, makes him out to be.

An Aristotelian ethical theory which downplays the role of activity in its formulation of the *telos* is surely one which taxes our ability to accept it as Aristotelian. But except for misguided critics of pleasure, no one in antiquity tried to push Hieronymus out of the school—there are no stories like those about the Stoic Diodorus the Renegade, who apparently had to be reclassified as an Epicurean because he took pain too seriously.[38] Hieronymus seems to have pursued a formulation or adaptation of Aristotle's notion of the goal of life that answers most directly to the appeal of Epicurean quietism—the notion that it is by avoiding difficulties and upset that one might most readily live a happy life. White[39] gets a sense of this when he contrasts Hieronymus's formulation with the reputation of Lycon for public service. Hieronymus, never a head of the school and innocent of any reputation for public service, might well have wanted to emphasize the quietistic aspect of the Aristotelian tradition.

The question of the relative value of the theoretical and the practical lives was one of the most persistent issues in ancient moral theory; it must have featured prominently in many of the works entitled *peri biōn*, and it was a major preoccupation of the Peripatetic Dicaearchus, who apparently disagreed with Theophrastus on the question.[40] Should one engage in the activities of a businessman, a citizen, even a political leader? Or should one avoid it all, keep a low profile, and cultivate one's rational virtues in the privacy of one's own home? Whatever Lycon's own view (and I am less sanguine than White that we can use the anecdotes about his life to guide our interpretation of his theory), it seems to me very likely that the key to understanding Hieronymus's innovative Aristotelianism lies here. Unlike so many of his fellow Aristotelians, including Lycon, Hieronymus preferred the nonparticipatory life which Epicureans also embraced.[41] It does not in the least follow that he had the same conception of what the sensible man should do with the free, undisturbed time that such quietism put at his disposal. Quite possibly Hieronymus would have been happy to take a more flexible, disjunctive position—one could do physics with Strato, mathematics with Eudoxus, or historical researches with Eudemus, all equally reasonable *bioi* to pursue. He need not have advanced the hedonistic ideal of Epicurus—not even in the Aristotelian version which Lycon apparently extracted from the hesitant accounts in Aristotle's own *Ethics*. And there need be nothing anti-Stoic in this either—even Chrysippus had to defend himself against charges of undue quietism;[42] Socrates himself had avoided the kind of public life which would cause him trouble—though he failed in this attempt and faced the ultimate *ochlos* and *tarachē* of a capital trial and execution.

Hieronymus, I suggest, can best be seen as taking a position on a particular, and by his day familiar, question in Aristotelian ethics—the relationship between the theoretical and practical lives. Once again, a neo-Aristotelian takes up a position of his own from among the options left open or at least unclear by the founder. It is indeed a bit shocking that Hieronymus didn't, as far as we can tell, even bother to emphasize the role of activity in his conception of the good life. But then, neither did his bête noire, Lycon. And perhaps too many of our own contemporary neo-Aristotelians don't do so either.

As many have noticed, including Julia Annas (whose 1993 book is the most philosophically persuasive account to date of this period), there seem to be two main drivers of change in Aristotelian ethics after Aristotle. First and foremost is surely the open-ended, sometimes incomplete condition in which Aristotle left much of his theorizing in the area. And second is the competitive pressure of philosophical debate, in particular with the Stoics. I want to close this chapter by questioning the somewhat narrow focus on Stoic influence which has characterized Annas's discussion and that of Stephen White—indeed, virtually all serious discussions of the topic to date. I suppose this is natural enough, given the shared pedigree of Stoics and Aristotelians—all roads lead back to Socrates and in this case both lead to Socrates via the same intermediary, Plato. But in the third century BCE Aristotelians faced other challenges too, and in particular challenges from the new and very active Epicurean school. About which, then, a word is in order.[43]

The general image of the Epicurean school is that of a withdrawn, quietistic group, drawing disingenuously on the Democritean tradition in physics and on the hedonistic tradition in ethics, generally tending its own intellectual garden and leaving well enough alone. But as applied to the first couple of generations after the founder, this seems to be a misguided view of its activity. Not only was Epicurus himself a controversialist and critic of other schools, but so especially was Colotes, about whom Plutarch makes us well informed. This is also true of other early Epicureans, such as Hermarchus. And even in later centuries we learn from scattered bits of Herculaneum papyri that Epicureans such as Zeno of Sidon were more actively involved in debating other schools than the traditional historiography recognizes. When Chrysippus, in the late third century, polarizes the main options in ethics between virtue and pleasure, he is certainly picking up a trend established in the fourth century with Xenophon,[44] but I don't think the head of the Stoic school in Athens wasted his time on debates with ghosts. Contemporary hedonists were almost certainly among his targets, and who were they if not Epicureans? So if we see, as we certainly do, a marked openness to hedonism among Aristotle's followers, we should surely think not only of Aristotle's own emphasis on the (admittedly subordinate) role of pleasure in the happy life, but also of the need to argue against and deal with contemporary, that is, Epicurean hedonism. Taking on board some of the plausible and appealing intuitions about human nature on which Epicureans also drew even as they developed a fresh version of Aristotle's ethics—this should not strike us as unlikely. In fact, we should probably take up the opportunity created by the late Marcello Gigante in one of his last works, *Kepos e Peripatos*,[45] and explore more intensively the two-way dialogue and debate between these schools in our period. We should recognize, then, that at least for a certain time Aristotelians would naturally be as concerned about Epicurean "competition" as about the Stoics.

But there is no doubt that in ethics this eventually ceased to be the case. By the time we get to Cicero, and then in Seneca,[46] Plutarch, Alexander, and in virtually the entire later ancient world, Epicureanism is decisively and effectively "bracketed out," even "silenced." As far as I can tell, the reason for this was a change in the terms of the debate created in part by the next major neo-Aristotelian philosopher, Critolaus of Phaselis, and by the influence of this change on all the major players in the debates of the first century BCE, including Antiochus of Ascalon and Cicero. In effect, then, there is a strong tendency in much current scholarship to close one's eyes to the hedonistic sympathies of early neo-Aristotelians and to the vigor of bilateral debate between Epicureans and Aristotelians; this, I suggest, is in part a result of being overly influenced by the "big picture" of ancient ethics which crystallized in Cicero's presentation and then settled in as the norm in later centuries. Cicero's work is, of course, *our* main source of information—almost everything else is lost—but in the ancient world more and more varied sources would have been available. But all, as far as I can see, conspire to tell the same story. Before I conclude this chapter, then, let me outline that story briefly.

From the first century BCE onwards, philosophy inhabited a new world, a Greco-Roman world. Whether they wrote in Latin or in Greek, Romans and Greeks who lived and worked in a Roman or Romanized environment shared their intellectual and cultural space. Cicero's close interaction with Greek philosophers is one clear sign of this. So are the presence of Greek philosophers at the imperial court of Rome, the philosophical connectedness of Seneca, the noticeable Romanness of Plutarch, the Greek philosophical diaries of the Roman emperor Marcus, Alexander's occupation of an imperially endowed chair of Aristotelian philosophy, the reliance of Plotinus on imperial patronage . . . and so forth. This is not a new story. But it is a story which begins, symbolically and (I will argue) actually in the mid second century BCE.

The story is certainly familiar: in 155 BCE Athens is on the wrong side of a potentially expensive diplomatic spat and sends her top philosophers to Rome to plead her case. These top philosophers are the heads of three schools, and three schools only: the Academy (Carneades from Cyrene in North Africa), the Stoa (Diogenes from Babylon, about twenty miles downstream from modern Baghdad), and the Peripatos (Critolaus from Phaselis in what is now southern Turkey). The geographical spread of their origins speaks volumes about the world that philosophy had come to inhabit; Athens drew in talent from all over the east. And then she sent it on to Rome as Rome gradually integrated itself into the culture it was rapidly absorbing. In addition to pleading in the Senate, these star intellectual visitors also gave public lectures. One at least, Carneades, spooked the aristocracy with his freewheeling political and ethical debate and the philosophers were abruptly sent home to Athens.[47]

For whatever reason, no Epicurean was present. This symbolizes—though perhaps this part is only symbolism—something of profound importance about later ancient ethics: there is a natural grouping of the three Socratic schools, one that persisted even as the Academy transformed itself from a seat of skepticism to a forum for Platonic doctrine. And Epicureanism is now officially and irrevocably the "other," the enemy. This configuration of debate is clearly represented in the structure and content of Cicero's *On Goals*, which (at least as far as we modern readers are concerned) plays an important role in the history of ancient Aristotelian ethics and in virtually every development in ethics for the rest of antiquity. This exclusion of Epicureanism persists in our contemporary treatments of ancient ethics, and my argument here is simply that though this may be true for most of antiquity, it is not true of the third century BCE; and that this matters for the history of Aristotelianism. However, what matters even more is what we turn to in the next chapter, the dramatic changes introduced into Aristotelian ethics by Critolaus, the most important voice in Aristotelian ethics between Aristotle himself and Alexander of Aphrodisias.

3

The Turning Point:
From Critolaus to Cicero

In the middle of the second century BCE the head of the Peripatetic school was Critolaus, without doubt the most powerful thinker to head the school in over a century. In Athens, the philosophical debate was rough and tumble. Carneades had breathed new life into the Academy, not only in epistemology (with his sustained critique of Stoic theory and his own developments of skepticism in the Academic tradition founded by Arcesilaus) but also in other branches of philosophy. Gisela Striker once elegantly dissected the debate between Carneades and the Stoic Antipater of Tarsus over the proper formulation of the *telos*;[1] Myles Burnyeat has tackled the interaction between these two in epistemology.[2] Antipater was the successor of Diogenes in the Stoic school, and while we are particularly well informed about Carneades's devastating onslaught against Antipater, we can safely assume that the charismatic Academic was just as stimulating a critic for Diogenes and Critolaus. Carneades stirred up the Stoics to refine and rework their formulations of the *telos*, the general effect of which was to clarify and sharpen the Stoic version of *eudaimonia* and also to make it more unambiguously "naturalistic" than perhaps it seemed in earlier Stoic versions.

Without bogging down in details, let me quickly illustrate what I mean by this. Diogenes's *telos* is "to be reasonable [*eulogistein*] in the selection [and rejection] of things which accord with nature" (SVF 3.44–46) and one definition of the good attributed to him (by Cicero in *On Goals* 3.33) emphasizes *natural* perfection and does not include any overt mention of a divine plan: *ego adsentior,* says Cato, *Diogeni, qui bonum definierit id quod esset natura absolutum.* "I agree with Diogenes, who defined the good as 'that which is perfected by nature'" or perhaps "completed with respect to nature." Antipater's *telos* is similarly naturalistic: either "to live selecting things that accord with nature and rejecting their opposites" or "doing everything in one's power, consistently and unswervingly, to acquire the most important things which accord with nature" (SVF 3.57–58). His definition of the good seems to have tied it (perhaps misguidedly) to the "reasonable selection of natural things" (SVF 3.59).[3]

Now these Stoics were unlikely to have been abandoning what they took to be the substance of Stoic ethics and they were certainly able to accommodate whatever Chrysippus himself had in mind when he said that the *telos* was living "in accordance with experience of what happens by nature."[4] And it is certainly not the case that all later Stoics jumped onto this bandwagon when deciding how best to formulate the goal of life (Posidonius, according to one of the same sources, Clement, said it was "to live contemplating the truth and order of the universe and to join in promoting it as far as possible, in no way being led by the irrational part of the soul"—all in all a more cosmically and hence theologically oriented expression of what is presumably the same basic idea). But there was nevertheless, in the mid second century BCE, a marked emphasis in Stoic theories on what is natural, and it was, I think, a result of Carneadean pressure on Diogenes and Antipater.

And no doubt the pressure was similar on the Peripatetics. For their leading light (and there was only one, though a couple of small fry do get mentioned as sharing some of his views[5]) shows similar inclinations. Critolaus took several bold positions in ethics, in the process setting the Aristotelian tradition in ethics on a novel trajectory that it would not abandon for over two hundred years. Not that Critolaus had narrow interests. The sources, such as they are, reveal serious interests in rhetoric, psychology, and cosmology as well, though conceivably he (like his Academic nemesis) published no book.[6] If true, this would help to account for the sense one gets that our understanding of him is entangled with the harmonizing project of Antiochus of Ascalon which dominates so much of Cicero's work on Greek ethics; as David Hahm has recently shown, the more closely one focusses on Critolaus, the stronger the suspicion becomes that Antiochus learned a very great deal from him, more than he was ever prepared to admit.[7] Before looking at his influential innovations in Aristotelian ethics, I'd like to sketch briefly what we know of Critolaus's general philosophical stance.

In physics he was not a slavish Aristotelian, but recognizably part of the tradition. The cosmos is eternal;[8] time is a sort of psychological measure, not a substantial being.[9] But according to one late source (Epiphanius 3.31 = fr. 15 Wehrli) he "followed Aristotle" in a number of views that *we* do not recognize as having been held by Aristotle: there were two *archai* of the cosmos, god and matter, providence governs the superlunary realm but not our region of the universe, which is governed by an irrational motion (*alogos phora*), the upper realm being indestructible but not the lower. On the nature of the soul we get mixed messages; Epiphanius claims that he shared the view of Aristotle that soul is an actuality of the body, but other sources[10] claim, more credibly, that Critolaus thought that the soul was corporeal, being made of extremely pure and refined *aithēr* or quintessence.[11] Rhetoric was not at the heart of Aristotle's philosophy, though it may have been the subject that mattered most to many of the statesmen who were drawn to Aristotle's school and to the dialecticians who practiced argument "on both sides of a question" (*in utramque partem*), as Cicero put it. For Aristotle, rhetoric is a full-fledged *technē*, a craft of persuasion with clear canons of method and standards of success. On this point Aristotle parted company with Plato, but despite the significance of that decision, Critolaus struck out on his own and denied rhetoric the status of a craft,[12] thereby aligning himself with the Socrates of Plato's *Gorgias*. Like Carneades and later Cicero, perhaps, Critolaus (fr. 24 Wehrli = Clement *Strom.* 2.7) attacked the Stoics for squabbling over words when they introduced allegedly new theories—they were deemed "word warriors," *onomatomachoi*, for having relied on stipulative terminology in the debate about the passions.

In ethics, though, Critolaus was a curious mixture of the conservative and the radical. As I argue elsewhere,[13] Critolaus crystallized into a firm doctrine the view that there are three kinds of goods *(tria genera bonorum);* of course, this general position had been held or at least proposed by Plato and Aristotle, alongside other views. But Critolaus faced off in debate with Stoics who argued vociferously that there is only one kind of good (virtue and what participates in virtue) and who even tried to foist this view onto Plato himself (Antipater wrote a book purporting to prove that "according to Plato only the *kalon* is good," thus coopting him to the Stoic viewpoint).[14] In this dialectical context, then, and no doubt influenced in part by Carneades's proneness to wield *divisiones* in his own philosophical critiques, Critolaus firmed up the view that all good things could be neatly categorized under the headings of body, soul, and externals. Again, I emphasize that the view itself is not novel; the essential move he makes is to convert it into a *dogma* around which debate would come to be organized.

And this categorization of the goods played a key role in Critolaus's innovative and influential moves in ethics. These moves, which I will come to in a moment, are by general agreement motivated by debate with the Stoics.[15] According to Clement (*Strom.* 2.21 = fr. 20 Wehrli) Critolaus held that the *telos* is the "completion [*teleiotês*] of a naturally smooth-flowing life," a formulation with echoes of Aristotle and clear citation of Zeno's *telos,* the smooth flow of life *(eurrhoia tou biou);* Clement also says, plausibly, that this is meant to indicate the "trigeneric[16] completion, filled out with all three kinds [of goods]." The key new term[17] here is *filled out* or *completely filled (sumplêrousthai),* and elsewhere[18] the *telos* is described as what is completely "filled out" by all the goods. By this he must mean to refer to all three *kinds* of goods rather than all the possible good things.

Given the prominence of the notions of actuality and activity in our thinking about what counts essentially as Aristotelian, it may be surprising to find a leading Peripatetic enunciating a theory of the goal of life which makes no explicit mention of activity;[19] but as we have seen, this is not without precedent among ancient neo-Aristotelians. The goods of the soul in question are virtues, not (as far as we can see) virtuous actions. And it is fascinating to see the theory positioned so sharply as a riposte to the Stoics. But the claim that happiness must be filled out with *all three kinds* of goods is perhaps the most significant feature of Critolaus's ethics. For it is surely an anti-Stoic move, natural and comprehensible in the context of the debates of his day. And it also takes up, without any apparent hesitation, one of the positions on the value of external and bodily goods that hovers about rather loosely in Aristotle's own ethical works. The questions of how, why, and to what extent one needs external goods such as wealth and bodily goods such as health are left tantalizingly unresolved in Aristotle, though there is no doubt that Aristotle himself gave the greatest weight to *activity* in accordance with rational excellence. Critolaus seems to have responded to that openness in Aristotle's own works with a clear resolution, the opposite resolution to the one which a Stoic would have chosen to adopt.

Now at this point one might, especially in view of our limited sources, suspect that the absence of any reference to activity is a mere accident and that Critolaus may well have been a better Aristotelian, in our sense, than I am alleging. But that cannot be so, for not only does Antiochus (who shares so many features of Critolaus's ethical stance, on which more later) show the same reticence, but we also have explicit criticisms of Critolaus (and those influenced by him) for omitting activity from their understanding of the *telos*. In Sharples's translation, one such source says:[20]

> By the younger Peripatetics from the school of Critolaus the end is said to be "what is *completed* from all the goods"—that is, from the three kinds of goods; but this is wrong. For not all good things are part of the end; bodily goods are not, nor are those derived from outside, but the activities of virtue in the soul alone. So it would have been better to say, instead of "completed" "activated" so that it might be apparent that virtue *employs*[21] these things.

Similarly, another early Imperial doxographer of the Peripatetic persuasion (whom we shall meet again shortly) sets the *dogma* of Critolaus aside as a definite mistake.[22]

> Since virtue greatly surpasses bodily and external goods both in what it produces and in being an object of choice on its own account, in

accordance with the argument that the end is not a completion made up out of [*sumplērōma ek*] bodily and external goods and is not a matter of gaining all of these; rather, it is to live virtuously with bodily and external goods, either all of them or most and the most important. So happiness is virtuous activity [*energeia*] in actions of a primary sort, as one would wish. Bodily and external goods are said to produce happiness because their presence makes a contribution; those who think that they *complete* [*sumplēroun*] happiness are ignorant, for happiness is a life, and life is *completed out of* action [*praxis*]. No bodily or external good is in itself either an action or an activity at all.

The evidence is pretty overwhelming, then, that Critolaus deliberately and self-consciously omitted the idea that activity in accordance with virtue was the core feature of the Aristotelian *telos*. Instead, he has adopted, perhaps reverted to, the idea that *having* goods is the key, and moreover that some amount of each kind of good is needed for a fully successful human life. (I say "reverted to" this position because the idea that happiness is a matter of possessing goods is a view one could claim as Platonic or even Socratic, since it is taken for granted in the *Symposium* at 205a1; in the *Euthydemus* the discussants begin, at 278e, from the presumably widespread view that happiness is the possession of good things and argue their way to the view that simply having goods is not enough, that using the goods you have is the key; see 281–282. The *Meno* too shows signs of this way of thinking about happiness at 87–89 and the idea is not unknown in Aristotle either.[23])

This move by Critolaus constituted a very influential reorientation of ethical debate. Not only did the Stoic Antipater find himself forced to concede to Critolaus that some externals are needed for happiness (see SVF 3.53 Antipater = Seneca *Ep.* 92.5), but, as we shall see shortly, the Peripatetics' fellow travelers in the first century BCE took the same position. This new view, that happiness was best understood as an aggregation of goods rather than as a pattern of excellent rational activity, actually *was* the core position of Aristotelian ethics for a long time, despite the reaction against it to which I have just alluded (and which can most plausibly be dated to the first century CE).

But the story is not quite this simple. For it seems that we need to recognize two further points about Critolaus, both of which also stuck in the tradition. First, despite the widespread recognition that pleasure is a natural condition, preferable or good as the case might be, the prevailing anti-Epicurean climate of debate clearly led Critolaus (like those who followed him in the next century) to reject pleasure as a component of the goal,[24] even arguing that it is a bad thing and the cause of further bad outcomes. In view of Aristotle's position on the relationship of pleasure to activity this is, in a way, not surprising: the neglect of activity in the formulation for the good life made possible a neglect, even rejection, of the pleasures which in Aristotle's own theories, both *Eudemian* and *Nicomachean,* attend upon it. But in view of how warmly some of his Aristotelian predecessors had embraced pleasure and freedom from pain, this move too should be seen as a sign of Critolaus's inclination to innovate. Changes in the dialectical climate may lie behind this development, and one can only speculate that the influence of Carneades and of anti-Epicurean argument among the Stoics may have played some role.

But second, and even more influential in the decades to come, Critolaus's views about the importance of possessing goods opens up quite explicitly a space for debate about the *weighting* of the various kinds of goods (and instances of them, in fact) in the happy life. And so we find Critolaus introducing perhaps his most famous image, the balance pans of the scale (surely derived ultimately from the scales of Zeus in the *Iliad* [8.68–78, 22.208–213] as much as from the famous passage in Plato's *Protagoras*, 356b, and from the realities of daily life in the market place). His motivation is pretty obvious. No one in the mainstream of the Socratic tradition is prepared to abandon the centrality and essential role of virtue itself; a happy life without at least the presence of virtue would, in fact, be an impossibility even for Epicurus (who regarded it as a necessary means for maximizing and preserving pleasure) and it seems to have been an uncontroversial constraint on all eudaimonist theories that virtue should play a key role. And yet the adoption of the doctrine that all three kinds of good are required for happiness, that one's life has to be "filled out" with these goods, seems to bring with it a recognition that virtue and the other goods of the soul are commensurable with the other kinds of good.

And if noncharacter goods are admitted to be the same in kind and so commensurable with virtue, what is to prevent it from being the case that one might have so much bodily good and so many external benefits that life counts as happy even when one's soul-goods are negligibly small? I might be as wealthy as Croesus and in glowing good health, a good health reinforced by the wealth I need to purchase the very best medical care, an elite personal trainer and membership at the best gym on the planet, the very finest athletic gear; but my mental goods are, well, modest. I'm sort of temperate, but a juicy steak and a bottle of fine merlot can always sway my resolutions; I'm reasonably good at geometry, but too lazy for algebra or calculus; I rather like the idea of learning languages and feel the inclination to be kind to small animals, but actually *acting on* these values seems to be far too much trouble. After all, what's in it for me, really? So I have some goods in each of the three categories and the overall package looks pretty attractive. How is this *not* a life according to nature? Why would this *not* be happiness, at least in the fortunate and privileged individual circumstances which make this set of choices possible?

Obviously, if we had clung to a traditional Aristotelian focus on activity in accordance with rational excellence then the issue wouldn't have come up. All we'd have to worry about would be the balance between different kinds of rational excellence (theoretical and practical) and one might even accept a kind of pluralism here. (No doubt we would also want to worry a bit about how vulnerable such a life might be to contingencies such as war, pestilence, and famine, but that's a problem common to both Aristotelian models of the happy life, since an Aristotelian activity-based account of the good life does require raw materials; only Stoics can claim invulnerability, though this comes at a high cost in plausibility.) This, however, is exactly the move which Critolaus does not and cannot make, given his conception of the good life as a *sumplērōsis*. So, how can he ensure that virtue plays a conventionally suitable role, the role demanded of it by our everyday moral intuitions?

The fact that goods are commensurable and indeed measurable at all is the source of the problem. Various goods can be weighed against each other, aggregated and subtracted according as the circumstances of life treat us well or badly. This situation clearly puts at risk what Stephen White has called the sovereignty of virtue,[25] and this vulnerability was in fact one of the sticks used most frequently to beat Epicurean consequentialism into submission. You *say* that one cannot live pleasantly without living virtuously and vice versa, but what is there to guarantee that outcome, aside from wishful thinking? Critolaus has, it seems, painted himself into the same corner. What to do? This is the motivation for the famous stipulation (for it can be no more than that) which Cicero cites and embraces in the *Tusculan Disputations* [5.51 = 18M Sharples].

> At this point I ask what is the power of those scales of Critolaus, who thinks that, when he puts the goods of the soul in one side of the

scales, those of the body and external ones in the other, the former will weigh more to such an extent that it will outweigh the earth and the seas? (tr. Sharples)

Theophrastus was open to criticism for giving too much weight to fortune and external contingencies, as was Epicurus. It is open to question whether this stipulation of relative weights is cogent—to me it is rather too much like having the butcher put his thumb on the scales—but it was certainly influential. Cicero's own attitude to it is sometimes hard to pin down, but later in the same book (5.75–76 = 18N) he is prepared to grant the legitimacy of the three kinds of goods *only* as a response to Stoicism and at that *only* if we grant that bodily and external goods have such a low weighting that they cannot possibly threaten the claim that goods of the soul, virtue, suffice for the happy life.

> As far as I am concerned, may the Peripatetics and the Old Academy eventually stop stammering and dare to say, openly and clearly, that there will be a happy life even in the bull of Phalaris. Let there be three kinds of goods, so that we can get out of the snares of the Stoics which I realise I have used more than usual; let there certainly be those kinds of goods, provided that bodily and external goods lie prostrate on the ground and are only called goods because they should be "taken," while those other divine goods [i.e., of the soul] spread far and wide and right up to the heaven; why should I say that the person who has obtained *these* is only happy and not also most happy? (tr. Sharples)

If Cicero was prepared to accept this view, which originated with Critolaus, at least sometimes and to some extent, that may well be a result of Peripatetic influence, almost certainly filtered through Antiochus's conception of what the Old Academy stood for.[26] For it is this view which dominates in the final book of the *On Goals*, in which Cicero has his main interlocutor, Piso, speak unambiguously for the Peripatetics on ethical questions.[27] And Piso assures us, against the Stoics, that

> it is right to say that these bodily advantages [=goods] have only small importance for the happy life; but it is too impulsive to say that they have none at all. Those who object to this point seem to me to forget *those very principles of nature* they themselves established. *Some* weight *must* be given to these goods, so long as you realize what the right amount is. (*On Goals* 5.72, tr. Woolf, my emphasis)

For Piso, spokesman for the Peripatetics on this question, the principles of nature, naturalistic principles for ethics, are inextricably linked to granting suitable weight to bodily and external goods in the calculus of the happy life.

Though embraced by later thinkers, Peripatetic and Academic alike (once the Academy had abandoned skepticism), this is clearly, in its origin, Critolaus's theory. And it represents an approach to eudaimonism which transforms the theory inherited from the great thinkers of the fourth century BCE. It addresses, once again, issues left open or unclear in Aristotle himself—such as the relationship between external goods and merely bodily excellences to virtue and happiness—and (if Cicero's assessment is accepted) it does so in a way which is less objectionable than Theophrastus's attempts to address it. Theophrastus, Cicero complains repeatedly, simply left too much to contingency; he was therefore quite unable to assure us that virtue would lead to happiness. In that Theophrastus was perhaps more candid (he did not put *his* thumb on the scale as Critolaus later did), but if our sources, his critics, are to be believed, he failed to secure what was regarded as the proper role for virtue. Critolaus (and his followers in the school, as well as his better-known Academic imitator Antiochus) did so, but apparently at a considerable cost in dialectical credibility.

Why pay such a high price? Why not assure the dominant role of mental goods in happiness simply by sticking with Aristotle's approach, based on activity rather than goods, on *doing* rather than *having*? No doubt the answer, if we could know it in full, would be complicated, and Critolaus's responsiveness to contemporary debates must be part of the story. I am confident that one explanation should be ruled out: I very much doubt that the cause was simple ignorance of Aristotle's theories, that Critolaus just didn't know what Aristotle had said on the topic. The old legend about the complete loss of the so-called esoteric works in the Hellenistic era has long been put to rest by a number of careful historical studies.[28] So I prefer to think of Critolaus as being deeply immersed in the contemporary debate—and that debate had come to focus on the possession of goods as the key to happiness. This was hardly a revolutionary idea: as we have seen, it is present in Plato's *Symposium* and so part of the shared inheritance of all the Socratic schools.[29] Aristotle and Plato both had a great deal to say about the proper categorization of the goods and their relationship to happiness—it must have been a focal point for discussion in Critolaus's own day (I am thinking again, here, of Antipater's book "that only the *kalon* is good according to Plato").

I think that a good case could be made for the idea that the famous *Carneadea divisio* also exercised considerable influence here. For one effect of the division, a dialectical tool for ordering and sifting what are supposed to be all possible theories of the *telos*, deployed with an eye to showing that all of them faced insuperable problems, was to flatten out the conceptual landscape. And when debates are structured by grand synoptic frameworks they are bound to miss out or deemphasize distinctive features of particular theories. That, no doubt, is why in his dialogue *On Goals* Cicero restricts the role of Stoic cosmology in his presentation of Stoic ethics; this facilitates debate and comparison among very different moral theories by setting up a common framework of debate.[30] But surely the same goes for the Carneadean framework.[31] In its various forms the Carneadean division omits all reference to kinds of activity as a component of the *telos*. The characteristic, uniquely distinctive Aristotelian feature of *telos* theory, the role of activity, was suppressed because it made impossible the kind of synoptic comparison needed for the *Carneadea divisio*.

The principal constraining assumption on which Carneades built was one characteristic of the debates of the Hellenistic era, that all the values which can be candidates for being the *telos* should be traceable to a naturalistic starting point in very young animals (this is the famous *oikeiōsis* theory or cradle argument).[32] And so pleasure, freedom from pain, and what the Stoics call "primary natural advantages" (roughly, bodily and external goods) are the main organizing values of the *divisio*, and for obvious reasons a concern with *to kalon* is added as being indispensable to a full account of all possible theories of the *telos*. I won't plunge into the details of how this dialectical tool was meant to work in the hands of Carneades, or how Cicero or anyone else exploited it. Annas, Algra, and others (not least Gisela Striker, in her Nellie Wallace lectures on "Following Nature"[33]) have done far more for this issue than I could hope to do. Rather, I would simply point out that none of the basic orienting values taken into consideration involve what is most essential to Aristotle's own distinctive theory—activity rooted in the basic nature of animal life, activity rooted in the network of capacities *(dunameis)* that for Aristotle just *are* the soul of an animal. This deep biological naturalism, which modern students of Aristotle intermittently attend to in the study of his ethics (though usually only when wrangling about the character of the function argument), has no place at all on the landscape of debate in the second century BCE. Even if Critolaus was keenly aware of Aristotle's biological naturalism and its potential relationship to ethics,[34] there would have been no plausible way to put that part of his theory to work in the context of contemporary debate. And that is not surprising, since everything else we know about Critolaus suggests that, for better or worse, he was a clear and perhaps somewhat limited representative of the dialectical conception of philosophy. More of an arguer than a theorizer in his own right, he would have found it very difficult to break out of the framework of current debates.

But in the end at least one Peripatetic did so. I want in the last part of this chapter to turn to what I think of as the most exciting and innovative development of this stage in the history of ethics after Aristotle. Recall that at *On Goals* 5.72 the Peripatetic speaker, Piso, says: "that these bodily advantages [=goods] have only small importance for the happy life; but it is too impulsive to say that they have none at all. *Those who object to this point seem to me to forget those very principles of nature they themselves established*" (*On Goals* 5.72, tr. Woolf, my emphasis). Piso, that is, here puts particular emphasis on the role of naturalism in the acceptance of the three kinds of goods. Anyone could see from even the most cursory observation of the natural world and its denizens that bodily and external goods are precisely the kinds of things which *all* animals feel drawn to (though of course what counts as a bodily or external good will vary depending on the animal species). Aristotle, in the *Nicomachean Ethics*, had rejected the form of argument which Eudoxus used to support his hedonism (all animals desire pleasure so pleasure must be *the* good). But this is a weaker and more plausible version of the basic idea. All animals desire x so x must be *a* good, not *the* good. And given the importance of controlling for cultural distortions in our conception of the good (an importance felt urgently not just by the sophists who distinguished *nomos* and *phusis* but also by Epicurus, Cynics, Plato, and others), it is a quite reasonable assumption that a value which is widespread in the animal kingdom must tell us *something* of importance about our own values, since we humans too are animals of a sort. And that insight underlies the use of the cradle argument by Peripatetics just as much as it supports Epicurean hedonism and Cynic antinomianism.

I have been saying, though, that the philosophical environment in which Critolaus worked was so structured that the basic Aristotelian insight (that some form of activity is the key to the *telos*) could not easily be introduced, that only the values recognized in the *Carneadea divisio* could be deployed, that this in fact was the main constraint on his very influential version of Aristotelian ethics. But I have also said that something happened to change that. Now, in concluding, we have to say what that was, and this will involve close attention to book 5 of Cicero's *On Goals* and to certain striking features of Piso's presentation of Aristotelian ethics. For it is Marcus Pupius Piso Frugi Calpurnianus, who for all his historical reality is here a mere character in Cicero's dialogue, who *re*introduces the key element of Aristotelian naturalism in ethics (universal and innate drives to activity) and integrates it into a persuasively naturalistic theory of ethics which once again includes the feature which we, or most of us anyway, think of as a key component of Aristotle's ethics.

Throughout the dialogue *On Goals*, several different versions of the cradle argument appear, and each is different in a manner suitable to the school represented. I have nothing particular to say about the Epicurean version here, but both the Stoic version in book 3 and the Peripatetic/Academic version in book 5 have distinctive and noteworthy features. First, the Stoic account offered by Cato differs from other Stoic versions in two ways: it emphasizes self-love rather than the mere drive to self-preservation (perhaps one might dismiss this as a mere presentational difference, though I don't think so myself); and second, Cato's account postulates a basic drive for the acquisition of knowledge which is fully parallel to the drive for self-preservation. The significance of these distinctive features in the Stoic account has been explored in a dissertation written by Ákos Brunner at the Central European University[35] and I hope that the results of his work will eventually be more widely available. But for present purposes the important Peripatetic novelties in Piso's account in book 5 should be set out briefly.[36]

Two features stand out as being of particular importance. First, there is a consistent and systematic emphasis on the comprehensiveness of the natural philosophy on which the ethics was based, starting with section 9 ("a great mass of material based on direct research is applied to the discovery of hidden realities" tr. Woolf [*maximam materiam ex rebus per se investigatis ad rerum occultarum cognitionem attulerunt*]). This involves botany as well as zoology. The fact that plants and not just animals are part of the story is first mentioned in section 10. After a typically Antiochean (that is, strongly partisan) review of earlier Peripatetics, the essentially Carneadean framework for reviewing moral theories is set out (16–23), and from there Piso proceeds to his version of the foundational cradle argument (24 ff.) but quite strikingly emphasizes in section 26 that the basic principles of this mode of analysis are found in *all* of nature, not just in animals. Plant life is specifically mentioned as working in the same way, so that Piso can then make a universal claim about all of nature without having to limit his generalizations to animals. The general claims about nature are based on an analogical unity, to be sure (*similem esse finem, non eundem:* see 25–26), but its inclusiveness reinforces the unambiguous integration of human behavior into this naturalistic mode of explanation: "from this you can grasp that the greatest human good is to live according to nature" *(ex quo intellegi debet homini id esse in bonis ultimum, secundum naturam vivere)*. Nor is this a fleeting commitment or mere hyperbole. Trees and plants recur in the argument at sections 33 and 39, and when Piso develops a thought experiment designed to reinforce the claim that every aspect of human behavior is governed by naturalistic principles, he begins the imaginative exercise with a plant (the grapevine)—more often in ancient ethics the compare-and-contrast game is played with humans and brute beasts. Not since Aristotle, if ever, have we seen such attention to the continuities between the principles of plant life (which are a form of soul) and human beings.

The other and in some ways more revealing new feature in Piso's account is his emphasis on precisely that aspect of Aristotelian ethics which we noted as being absent in Critolaus's theory, the intrinsic drive for activity. For not only is his entire account permeated with an emphasis on the dynamic and developmental character of the natural world, but there is an unmistakably Aristotelian emphasis on the *actualization* of the natural potentials of each species, and indeed of each significant part of each species. In section 35 our body parts are considered as functional subsystems of the whole animal; Piso emphasizes their teleological nature and the importance of their being unimpaired so that they can carry out their "natural movements and activities" *(naturales motus ususque)*. The sense organs have a natural function to fulfill *(munere fungatur* in section 36) as does every other natural component of the body. This is already a more Aristotelian kind of naturalism, though of course it is set within an argumentative context derived from debate with the Stoics.[37] The natural drive to *know* and *learn* is emphasized here (e.g., in section 48) as frankly as it is in the opening sentence of Aristotle's *Metaphysics,* but such a drive to actualization is in fact more general—all natural capacities display this characteristic. This is made explicit in sections 54–58, where there are abundant reminiscences of this aspect of Aristotle's own thought. Sleep is only for the sake of activity, and it would otherwise seem unnatural ever to cease being active. All human beings, though it is especially clear in children, are in constant activity *(aliquid semper agere)*; the difficulty that children have in ever sitting still is just a particularly clear manifestation of what nature as a whole is like (it is worth pointing out that it is only here, at 5.55, that the canonical reference to cradles, which gives the argument form its name, appears). But it is not a childish trait that we grow out of: the desire for activity *(cupiditas agendi)* grows as we grow, and even the people we stigmatize as lazy are actually always doing something (section 56).

The human drive for activity comes out either in a commitment to the life of the mind or to political labors (section 57), the former being "divine" in just the same sense that Aristotle said it was.

> Thus the more able and accomplished one is, the less one would even want to live at all if prevented from going about one's business, however well provided one may be with pleasures to graze on. One chooses either a life of private pursuits, or, if more ambitious, aspires to a public career and the authority of office. Alternatively, one devotes oneself entirely to intellectual study, a life far removed from that of the pleasure-seeker. Indeed, those who take this course endure worry, anxiety, and sleeplessness as they exercise the cutting edge of their talent and intellect, the finest element in a human being, and one that should be considered divine. Such people have no desire for pleasure nor any aversion to hard work. Indeed, their activity is ceaseless, be it wondering at the discoveries of the ancients or undertaking original research. Their appetite for study is insatiable. They forget everything else and never undertake a mean or unworthy thought. Such, indeed, is the power exerted by these pursuits that even those who claim to

have a quite different highest good, defined for example by utility or pleasure, may yet be seen to spend their whole life in the investigation and exposition of nature. (tr. Woolf)

The conclusion, then, that we are born for activity (*natos ad agendum*, section 58), could not be more markedly Aristotelian. And this natural and inevitable fact about human beings is put to use to support the claim that *all* of our characteristic behavior patterns are *natural*, that these are our specific, that is, species-relative functions. The term *munus* had been used for a similar point above at 5.36, so although Woolf is overtranslating slightly at 5.60 when he adds the term "function" to his translation (the Latin simply has *nostrum est*), he certainly captures quite effectively the Aristotelian flavor of the passage.

This account, then, is much closer to Aristotle's form of naturalism than what we saw in Critolaus. Even the negative stance towards pleasure in the texts I have emphasized has to be balanced out by Piso's acknowledgement of the pleasure taken in fulfilling a natural function (see sections 45, 48, 50–52) such as learning. What we see in Piso's speech, then, is a significant Aristotelian version of ethics, richly infused with the systematic naturalism that many think of as Aristotle's calling card. But whose theory is it? Who is responsible for this very significant stage in the tradition of ethics after Aristotle?

Clearly, not Critolaus. Although many features of the story in *On Goals* 5 owe a good deal to him, such as the emphasis on the *tria genera bonorum*, the problem of the thumb on the scale at 5.72, and the distinction between what is sufficient for a happy life and for the happiest life (itself an attempt to capture one of Aristotle's own ambivalences), this is not his theory. For it embraces a much wider range of biological phenomena, emphasizes the relationship of natural philosophy with ethics that goes far beyond the dialectical positioning characteristic of

Critolaus, and moreover this account begins by condescendingly con-
textualizing Critolaus within the history of the school—in 5.14 he
comes off very well compared to Hieronymus and Diodorus, but still
falls short of the "teachings of his ancestors." So who? Well, although
this is an Aristotelian theory, the likeliest candidate is . . . is it Antiochus
himself? Perhaps so, since he is emphatically identified as Piso's teacher.
It would be no surprise if Antiochus pulled in this Aristotelian material
and claimed it for his own, and it is clear that Platonic philosophers in
the Roman Empire, such as Plutarch and Alcinous, were ready enough
to absorb Aristotelian doctrine into their own philosophical amalgam.
Antiochus would simply be the pioneer in this process. In the past
(including my own past[38]) this has often seemed to be the most plausible view, but despite the many attractions of this hypothesis[39] we may
well have our doubts. Antiochus is surely one of Cicero's sources, but
surely he need not be reliant on only one source for Piso's speech.

And on reflection it seems that the philosopher who lies behind this
version of Aristotelian ethics need not be Antiochus, not least because
of the many ways in which Antiochus actually followed Critolaus's
lead in ethics, as we have seen. The truth about the origin of this striking version of Aristotelian ethics, no doubt, lies hidden forever in the
secrets of Cicero's authorial tactics, but two short passages in book 5
raise a concrete possibility. At the beginning of the book Cicero, the
character, justifies putting Piso on the spot to speak.

> My cousin Lucius is keen to find out the view of the Old Academy
> that you mention, and also of the Peripatetics, on the question of the
> highest goods. We think that you are the one to explain them most
> fluently, since Staseas of Naples has been a member of your household
> for many years, and we know that you have been pursuing the same
> topic with Antiochus in Athens these past few months. (5.8 tr. Woolf)

And at the end of the account the mysterious Staseas returns. Cicero again is speaking:

> Your speech won my approval all the more because Staseas of Naples, your teacher and a Peripatetic of unquestionably high repute, used to give a somewhat different account of the system. He would side with those who gave importance to fortune good or bad, and to bodily goods and evils.

To which Piso replies:

> Quite so . . . but our dear Antiochus gives a much better and bolder account of these matters than Staseas did. (5.75 tr. Woolf)

Several interpretations are possible. Since the tougher-minded position on the sufficiency of virtue for happiness is associated with Antiochus (it is something he inherited from Critolaus, like him being engaged in close argument with the Stoics), and since Cicero here seems to attribute to Staseas a weaker position that allows more weight to the contingencies that afflict external and bodily goods (that is, a position closer to Theophrastus[40]), it is possible that Staseas is the philosopher who pulled together the main account, with its richly Aristotelian version of ethical naturalism,[41] while Antiochus is responsible for the tougher and more Stoic-sounding stance on the sufficiency thesis. That would cohere with everything else we learn about Antiochus from Cicero and would also explain why Staseas, otherwise little known,[42] is even mentioned here. And if this is so—a view which I hope the reader will at least entertain seriously—it would mean that the overall author of Piso's account, now revealed as a composite of Aristotelian naturalism and Antiochean rigorism, is Cicero himself.

4

Bridging the Gap: Aristotelian Ethics in the Early Roman Empire

Disagreements about periodization are inevitable, but eventually the Hellenistic era came to close and a new era in philosophy began. I incline to include in the earlier period Cicero and the flowering of philosophical activity in Italy before the upheavals of the 40s and 30s BCE, not drawing a line at 100 BCE as some have recently proposed.[1] Both division points are defensible; whichever is chosen, it is clearly the case that by the 30s BCE, and with the beginnings of a transition to the new intellectual culture of the empire, the Aristotelian tradition in ethics would change too, in harmony with the kind of larger forces that shape social, literary, and even philosophical life. Philosophically, these developments culminate in the outstandingly creative career of Alexander of Aphrodisias, a small portion of whose work will be the main topic of our final chapter. But in the time between Cicero and Alexander enormous changes took place in the intellectual landscape and these had a considerable impact on the nature of ethics after Aristotle.

Though Alexander's independent-minded approach to doing ethics after Aristotle has certainly been influential and is probably the most intellectually rewarding aspect of the tradition, the centuries leading up to Alexander were characterized by a rapidly developing sequence of philosophical developments. I cannot hope to cover all of it, and will not try to emulate the synoptic work done by Moraux (1973–2001) and Gottschalk (1987) nor to replace the detailed studies by Sharples (including those in Sharples and Sorabji 2007), but a handful of significant issues can be explored. One of these is the striking fact that Aristotelians came, in the period after Critolaus and perhaps especially in the period after Antiochus, to view Stoics as their main opponents—or perhaps it was the Stoics who chose to oppose Aristotelians. Either way, the debate became intense, not least on the topic of the nature of the passions. But the debate between Aristotelians and Stoics was not confined to the passions; in Seneca we see a more general engagement with Aristotelian ethics, as he determinedly carves out space for a distinctive Stoic approach in the ever more crowded philosophical landscape of the early empire. For both on the topic of the passions (where Seneca's *On Anger* provides a vivid if one-sided image of contemporary debate with the Peripatetics) and on the theory of the good and the definition of the *telos* (which forms the subject matter of a sequence of letters in the *Letters to Lucilius*) we can get a rare firsthand view of contemporary debates between Stoic and Aristotelian philosophers. Interestingly, when we think of what Seneca's works tell us about the philosophical environment in Rome it seems quite clear that in ethics Aristotelianism really was the main debating partner, while Platonism, then in the midst of its own vigorous revival, had its impact more in metaphysics and physics. No doubt one could go further and explore how it came to pass that the Stoic Epictetus adopted the Aristotelian term *prohairesis* as a central principle in his own ethics,[2] or how later Aristotelians twisted and turned in their efforts to find just the right way to deal with the topic of pleasure—so important in Aristotle's ethics but so touchy in the Hellenistic world and after. But my space is limited, and choices have to be made.[3]

Somewhat later, with Plutarch, Alcinous, Atticus, and other Platonic authors, we can see the beginnings of the creative interaction between Aristotelian philosophy and Platonism that eventually concluded, after Alexander and Plotinus, with Platonists becoming the guardians, in effect, of the Aristotelian legacy. Some Platonists of the early empire creatively absorbed key features of Aristotelian ethics; others, most notably Atticus, vigorously rejected this tendency. But they all, virtually without exception, dealt with the legacy of ethics after Aristotle.

As the general histories of Moraux 1973–2001, Gottschalk 1987, and Sharples 2007 show, throughout the Imperial period Aristotelians display a growing tendency to focus on commentary, defensive explication, and the exegesis of Aristotle's texts, rather than on the sort of direct dialectical exchange which I have argued was characteristic of Aristotelianism in the Hellenistic period. The earliest commentaries, written in the late Hellenistic period, focused on the *Categories,* but the first *surviving* commentary is much later, from the pen of Aspasius. This professional philosopher wrote a commentary on Aristotle's *Ethics,* indeed, on the *Nicomachean Ethics;*[4] sadly, it does not survive entire, but we have enough to confirm that by his day, in the second century CE, commentary on the founder's texts had become the primary mode of philosophical work within the school (though as Alexander's corpus reminds us, this was certainly not the only mode).

The first emergence of commentaries on the master's works and critical engagement with them occurred in the context of a more general scholarly engagement with Aristotle's works and doctrine. Perhaps the clearest illustration of this can be found (or perhaps one should say, divined) in the remains of the works of Xenarchus of Seleucia, which can now be dated with some confidence to the late first century BCE. Andrea Falcon[5] has recently used our limited but invaluable evidence about Xenarchus to anchor an excellent general sketch of the state of Aristotelianism in the late first century BCE and the early first century CE.

From this same period two other Aristotelian ethical works survive which could be used to help tell the story of the transition between the Hellenistic and Imperial phases of Aristotelian ethics.[6] Both the pseudo-Aristotelian treatise on *Virtues and Vices* and the treatise *On the Passions* attributed to Andronicus of Rhodes (which itself includes a further adaptation of the pseudo-Aristotelian treatise) show signs of a similar late Hellenistic or early Imperial context.[7] The latter in particular is unmistakably entangled with Stoic theories of the passions and builds on the crisp dichotomy between *logos* and *pathos* that we first saw clearly in the *Magna Moralia* and which then became a common feature of Aristotelian theory. The treatise on *Virtues and Vices* would also repay closer analysis than it often gets, not only for its adaptations of Aristotle's theory to what I take to be the late Hellenistic environment but also for its explicit adoption of Plato's tripartition of the soul (an issue on which Aristotle himself displayed some ambivalence). Such openness to Platonic formulations had arguably been a feature of the *Magna Moralia* too, and this treatise, like its Platonist counterpart, Plutarch's *On Moral Virtue*, could profitably be treated as an early chapter in the story of Platonic/Aristotelian interaction in later antiquity.[8]

What can we learn from all of this about the general intellectual environment for Aristotelian ethics in the early empire? Even as commentary became more and more the main vehicle for new philosophical work, a great deal of debate, polemic, and cross-fertilization

among all three schools persisted; the results were a gradually growing creative fusion between Platonic and Aristotelian doctrines, a
persistent polarization between both of those schools and the Stoics
(reflected in Alexander's attacks on Stoic theories of determinism and
Stoic physics), and the radical silencing of Epicureanism—just as one
might have predicted from the prophetic philosophical configuration
of the Athenian embassy in 155 BCE, which sent an Academic, an
Aristotelian, and a Stoic to Rome. No Epicurean was asked to speak
to the newly dominant regional power, the Roman Senate, on behalf
of Athens, and it is noteworthy that from that point on Epicureans
were the philosophical outsiders; the other three schools could have
their debates and even quarrels, but Epicureans were usually beyond
the pale.

We concluded our last chapter with Cicero, and his works provide
us with the starting point for two of our themes, the conflict over
the nature of the passions and the differing approaches taken to the
naturalistic foundations of ethics in the Aristotelian and Stoic schools
in the so-called cradle argument. Our narrative begins with a symbolically appropriate transition figure, the author of a work known to
historians of philosophy as Doxography C (so called only because it is
the third in a sequence of doxographical accounts of ethics preserved
in book 2 of the *Anthology* of Stobaeus). The author of Doxography C
is often thought to be the man we think we know as Arius Didymus.[9]
But that identification is neither certain nor particularly important to
the story (except that *if* he is who we think Arius Didymus was, he
enjoyed the patronage of Augustus Caesar,[10] thus neatly anticipating
the situation of Alexander, who also enjoyed Imperial patronage). If
the author was not Arius then we have no idea who he was; and there
would also be something quite appealing in having another cardinal
text in ethics after Aristotle remain anonymous—as does the *Magna*

Moralia, which was the first major stop on our journey. The school's corpus incorporated an unusual number of anonymous or unattributable works, often preserved under Aristotle's name, as though (reasonably enough) it really is the content that matters, rather than the author; one may think of including pseudonymous works in the corpus as a strategy for preservation during a time when only "great men" mattered, rather than as bearing the stigma of inauthenticity.[11]

Doxography C is a curious work, and given the uncertainty about whether the author really was Arius Didymus, I am inclined to baptize its unknown author "Harry," to avoid encouraging too strong a presumption about his identity while at the same time avoiding the alienating effect of calling him "Anonymous" or "pseudo-Somebody." An artificial name at least fosters the sense that he was a real philosopher with interests and his own style of work.[12] But the peculiarities of the work speak for themselves, whoever the author was. It seems, in the last analysis, to be a compilation, but one that has been developed into a reasonably unified whole. The author, "Harry," combines paraphrase and discussion of Aristotle's own ethical works with doctrines derived from unmistakably Hellenistic developments in the school. At least, that is how he begins. By the end of the work it is a different story, as we shall see.

With Harry's treatise, which seems to have been composed around the time of Xenarchus or shortly after,[13] we are clearly in the very early stages of the development of the scholarly and commentarial mode of philosophical work. The work presents itself as a freestanding treatise in the Aristotelian mode, heavily dependent on paraphrase and summary of Aristotle's own texts (though not in the way the *Magna Moralia* was). It opens (chapter I) with a preface explaining the significance of the name of the discipline (ethics from *ethos,* following Aristotle very closely[14]) and of the importance of the pair reason/passion as a foundation for ethical enquiry. The starkness of this latter pairing is of course familiar from the *Magna Moralia* and was less apparent in Aristotle's own work. In chapter 2 the familiar Aristotelian partitioning of the soul is set out (depending on *Nicomachean Ethics* I.13 and other texts), but incorporating (as did the *Magna Moralia*) the Stoic terminology of *hormē* which had become common in the theories of the Hellenistic world. In chapter 3 the author moves with breath-taking speed from the traditional triad, accepted by Aristotle (*Eudemian Ethics* I.1), of *phusis, ethos,* and *logos* as factors in ethics, to the unmistakably Hellenistic theory of *oikeiōsis*[15] as a foundation for it. The similarities to the Peripatetic account in *On Goals* 5 have long been observed, though direct dependence on that work seems unlikely. This fresh starting point, or *archē,* as Aristotle himself would have put it, sets the treatise on an important new track from which it only diverges when straightforward paraphrase of Aristotle's treatises returns late in the work (at chapter 28), with development of the theme of moral virtue; it then continues in this vein to the end, though the last section is based on the *Politics* rather than on the ethical treatises.[16]

Instead of spreading ourselves thin enough to touch on all of these themes, I prefer to focus on Harry's approach to the question of how theories of morality are related to more or less naturalistic accounts of human nature and behavior,[17] for it is on this issue (rather than with other aspects of Aristotelian ethics) that we in the modern context still have most to learn from ancient Aristotelians (if only in the form of pertinent cautionary tales). And it is this theme that we will pick up in the work of Alexander in our final chapter. Now the place of naturalism, broadly conceived, in Aristotle's own ethics is controversial. There is, of course, a teleological and biologically grounded approach to ethics which underlies many aspects of the *Nicomachean Ethics.* Humans, like other animals, have a natural function, a teleological nature which not only explains but also justifies. From Aristotle's own naturalism we learn that the goal of a human being is to be understood in light of its characteristic function (*NE* I.7). And "characteristic" is the key word—it is for some reason our *distinctive* capacities, not those we share with other living things, to which we are supposed to look when filling in the detailed account of happiness. What is distinctive is, of course, our rationality, and so it is activity in accordance with excellence of our rational capacities which Aristotle claims as the central feature of human happiness or thriving.

It is worth reflecting for a moment on the appropriate reaction to Aristotle's general approach on this point—the more so, since it continued to be important for Aristotelians in the ancient world. One might, of course, embrace the general position but still disagree with Aristotle about what the human rational capacities are. Or one might embrace it and yet find that, in circumstances and in social conditions that Aristotle did not envisage, the exercise of those distinctive rational capacities requires different necessary and facilitating conditions than he imagined. In fact, one might very well accept the general program of thinking things through in ethics that Aristotle offers us without in fact embracing his detailed results. In that way we could learn a great deal from Aristotle's ethics by embracing his *style* of naturalism and yet not be just repeating his conclusions. However close we stay to Aristotle's own particular expression of this brand of naturalism, in opting for a naturalism of this kind we would not only be setting ourselves against various forms of supernaturalism in ethics (such as a divine command theory about what is right) and against various irrationalisms (such as a strong intuitionism about the good), but we would also be in a better position to avoid cultural relativism and various kinds of localism and ethnocentrism. Such variable, and therefore suspect, value commitments had been held up to skeptical scrutiny in the sophistic contrast of convention *(nomos)* and nature, but here we would find a concrete and presumably non-question-begging way of establishing the relevant characteristics of nature.

This is a program in ethics that appeals greatly to many people today, and it also appealed greatly to those who practiced ethics after Aristotle, despite the awkward fact that Aristotle himself seems not to have adhered consistently to his own naturalism (at least not the kind of naturalism reflected in the strategic use of appeals to the basic nature of each species rather than to a more grand and often theologically tinged naturalism that postulates purposes and plans in nature as a whole). It is no secret that in parts of his corpus[18] Aristotle himself shows some inclination towards global teleology and divine order as he leans towards a view of nature's role that originates with the *Timaeus,* perhaps, and that is certainly most characteristic of Stoicism. These inclinations of course put his basic naturalistic position (which focuses on the nature of each kind of animal rather than on the nature of the whole world) under some strain. Even more disturbing, it is hard to deny that Aristotle sometimes simply assumes that an essentially homologous relationship between human and divine reason plays a critical role in determining the best activities for a human being. This enables him to hold in *Nicomachean Ethics* book 10 and elsewhere that it is precisely in becoming more aligned with the *divine* and its characteristic activities that we are most intensely and appositely human. Emulation of the divine and "siding with the immortal" *(athanatizein* at *NE* 1177b3) are not quite as embarrassing for the naturalist as the Platonists' *homoiōsis theōi* would be, but it is an issue to be faced by those who find in Aristotle a model for naturalistic ethics. The issue is difficult, even though Aristotle emphasizes that the divine activity that we are to emulate is thinking—which sounds very much like a distinctive feature of human nature. But unlike human thinking, god's thought is not the activation of a capacity and has no object beyond its own pure and nondynamic activity. No account of human theoretical intellect could have those features, if left to its own devices. The kind of reason needed for this feature of the human *telos* is not a natural or human rationality.

Aristotelians after Aristotle did develop a theory that was better integrated into a naturalistic framework. In my view the most important case of this is the Aristotelian theory of *On Goals* 5 we considered in the previous chapter; in Cicero's presentation, Piso attempts to base his theory of the good life and virtue directly and exclusively on a theory of human nature validated not just by the Stoically influenced cradle argument, but by analogies drawn from an analysis of *all* living things, plants as well as animals. I concede that Cicero (the Academic skeptic) allows his readers to wonder how successful the finished product was, and (as so often in ancient ethics) there is a *pro forma* concession to the idea that our reason is linked to the divine. But in Piso's account there is no sign that this is doing any serious work, and in this it differs from the situation in Aristotle himself.

In the previous chapter I also suggested that the least persuasive feature of Piso's story (the attempt to retain the sufficiency of virtue for happiness despite the naturalistic recognition that we and our capabilities are vulnerable to external contingencies) should be attributed to Antiochus (who was excessively influenced by the commitment to debate against the Stoics which Critolaus took up so vigorously).[19] And if that is so, then we still can see in the rest of Piso's account a deep and systematic naturalistic basis for ethics which could frankly incorporate the rather depressing thought (about which Aristotelians since Theophrastus had been ambivalent) that human happiness is in fact very fragile, vulnerable to the contingencies and woes of the natural world. In my view, this realism turns out to be both a source of strength for a broadly Aristotelian ethics and at the same time its Achilles' heel.

Against this background, let's turn now to consider the work of our early Imperial neo-Aristotelian, Harry. How is our mature, adult conception of success as human beings related to our nature, a nature which is fundamentally analogous to the natures of all other species (even plants, if we want to go all the way with Piso)? Let me quickly go through the relevant aspects of Harry's treatise; we will return to some of these issues in our final chapter in connection with Alexander.[20]

Harry begins his account of human nature (at section 3) with an admission that humans "are different from other animals in both body and soul"—significant since the distinctive traits of humans are the ones pertinent to ethics—"because, since they are situated between immortals and mortals, they share a linkage with both: to the rational in virtue of what is divine in their soul and to the irrational in virtue of what is mortal in their body." This sharply expressed duality is clearly the key to an ethics which takes it starting point in human nature. What follows from this is clear: a human being "reasonably desires the perfection of both [soul and body]." But how does this fact about our nature turn into a desire? This, it turns out, is the critical move. It is a move which starts out from Aristotle himself, who held that we, like other living things, have a fundamental desire to exist,[21] and then adopts the characteristically Hellenistic language of *oikeiōsis*. A human being's:

first desire is to *be*, for by nature he is attached [*ōikeiōsthai*] to himself, which is why he is also suitably pleased by things that accord with nature and annoyed by things that conflict with it. He is keen to attain health, has a drive for pleasure and strives to live because these things are in accord with nature and worth choosing for themselves and good.

Contrariwise, he fights off and avoids illness, pain, and destruction because they are in conflict with nature and worth avoiding for themselves and bad. For our body is dear to us and so is our soul, and so too are their parts, their capacities and their activities; it is our planning for the preservation of these which is the starting point for impulse, appropriate action [*kathēkon*], and virtue. *For if absolutely no error ever occurred in the pursuit and avoidance of the aforementioned things, but if we hit upon the good ones and stayed free of the bad ones consistently, then we would never have undertaken to seek correct and error-free selection in connection with them.* But since we were in fact often misled in our pursuit and avoidance of them, sometimes passing over good things and embracing bad things as though they were good, it was necessary for us to seek out a reliable knowledge of how to distinguish them; when we also found that this was harmonious with nature we labeled it "virtue" because of the splendor of its actuality and, being wonderfully impressed by this, we came to honor it more than anything else. For it has turned out that rational actions [*praxeis*] and what are called "appropriate actions" take their starting points from selecting things that accord with nature and rejecting things that conflict with it. And that is why correct actions [*katorthōseis*] and mistakes occur in connection with them [appropriate actions] and are involved with them. For pretty much the entire framework of our school has its starting point from these factors, as I will demonstrate very concisely.

This text, admittedly written rather clumsily, is saturated with the Stoicized language of Hellenistic theory. Its basic strategy is clear. The context is established as Aristotelian right at the outset. The dual nature of human beings (body and soul, poised between beast and god) is proclaimed, and then the fundamentally natural character of the resultant motivations (accompanied by pleasure, of course) is laid out as a consequence of a basic commitment to our own existence, and not just our mere existence but to our being what we are in accordance with our basic nature. Strikingly, in contrast to Piso's account, we don't have a cradle argument here. The radical desire to *be* what we are is not just a fact about newborns; rather, it holds throughout life.

This is a significant change from the way the Epicureans, Stoics, and Piso chose to connect values to nature. Two consequences follow. First, without a cradle argument this account is vulnerable to charges that the values that allegedly motivate us have actually been socially inculcated and so may not be reliable guides to our underlying nature; but second, the very difficult issue of how one makes the transition from having the values of a non- or pre-rational animal to those of rational adult humans is avoided. Despite the similarity of some of the theoretical terminology here, the differences between Harry's theory of *oikeiōsis* and the earlier version should not be downplayed, especially as they affect the argumentative support for the doctrine and its general explanatory impact. Why, then, the changes? I think it very likely that, at this point in the history of the debate, this kind of *oikeiōsis* had pretty much come to be taken for granted as a relevant basic fact, and the cradle argument was no longer needed to support it in argument with other schools. And in the paragraphs which follow, Harry reinforces the naturalness of the network of motivations that underpin Aristotelian ethical principles in further ways that Aristotle himself would have approved of: by appealing to various *endoxa* we have about love for our offspring, feelings of kinship to others in our community, and so forth.

Harry declares that the *entire* framework (the word is *hupographē*) of Aristotelian ethics proceeds *(hōrmēsthai)* from this starting point, which seems to be more than a little hyperbolic.[22] No doubt, though, he meant to focus on some fairly basic aspect of ethics as being the key desideratum. And I think we can see how it was meant to work. Harry is addressing a challenge about ethical motivation. *Why* would we want to act virtuously? Fundamentally, because we desire our own existence, and that existence takes the form of our actually being a set of capacities that exist all the more strongly when they are developed and which ultimately are fulfilled by being actualized.[23] This is, of course, a somewhat Stoicized way of putting an Aristotelian point about desire and motivation. The teleological assumptions which do so much of the work are not under debate, and specific content is given to the desire by an explication of how practical reason actually works (practical reason in the form of selection and rejection of the natural goods and evils of body and soul, both of which are dear to us by nature since we just *are* our body and soul). All of this, as we saw earlier, seems to be a way of interpreting *phronēsis* that entered the Aristotelian tradition from Stoicism in the debates of the second century BCE.

The account of virtue's foundations is naturalistic not just because of its starting point in a form of *oikeiōsis* and because our selections are for natural goods, such as health and freedom from pain, that no one would seriously question. Harry also claims that, as we attempt to get things right, we *simply discover* that "reliable knowledge" is what we need and what we pursue in order to satisfy our basic desires. And once we learn this by experience, we come to see that it fits right into the quite familiar process of using practical reason to pursue goods; "virtue," then, is just the label we apply to this excellence of practical reason in pursuit of natural goods, applied as an honorific since we find it worthy of our respect and honor. This process is portrayed as being one of inevitable realization—we simply come to see that reason is the key to getting our natural goals and we label its excellence "virtue." It spontaneously evokes our admiration, since it is an effective way of coming to acquire the good things we want to get to fulfill our natural desires. The purportedly experiential basis for this elevation of practical reason is modeled on a move made by the Stoics—we may compare Cato's account of the purportedly natural emergence of our appreciation for how well things fit together as we cultivate a consistent use of reason in *On Goals* 3.21–23.

This is not mere eclecticism. Wrapped up in this dense but still somewhat under-argued passage is a whole theory of the basis for key aspects of a moral theory. It is an original and updated version of Aristotelian ethics, or at least the key bits which allegedly get it off the ground, and the rest of the work purports to show that everything relevant—including the nature and desirability of practical reason—follows from these natural principles. One of the more interesting features of Harry's account, which reflects its engagement with Stoic versions of the theory of *oikeiōsis*, is the way he portrays the rational agent as moving on after the initial appreciation of virtue, by which he appears to mean practical reason, *phronēsis*, as a means to acquiring the natural goods of the body and soul. At the next stage the agent seems to reflect on this newly discovered virtue and comes to see an additional and even more important value in it.[24] As he says, "when we also found that this was harmonious with nature we labeled it "virtue" because of the splendor of its actuality and, being wonderfully impressed by this, we came to honor it more than anything else." It is more than a little like the move that Cato makes in book 3 of *On Goals*, as I indicated above. In the Stoic account we come to value the order and harmony of our pattern of rational selections more than the selections themselves. So too for Harry: he thinks that our initial basis for being motivated towards virtue is of one sort, a virtually instrumental motivation for the exercise of practical reason; but at a second stage, about which Harry says surprisingly little, we come to see an additional value, and an even greater value, in this virtue. Both the initial account of how virtue is motivated and the subsequent stage of our appreciation for it might seem implausible as reflections on Aristotle's theory, but they fit well into the very different context defined by debate with the Stoics, without thereby losing their character as Aristotelian.

The argument in Harry's account is heavily focused on "starting points"—that is, *archai*.[25] This indicates that, in the eyes of those constructing this new version of Aristotelian ethics, the most pressing issue to deal with was not the fine points of what makes a virtue virtuous or what role is played by pleasure, or how contemplation fits into the practical life, where friendship fits, or even the nature of the passions. Rather, what had to be dealt with was the challenge of providing a naturalistic account of the basic motivation that underlies the rest. It was to be an account that linked ethics to the biological teleology that was recognized as characteristic of Aristotelian thought. It was cast in Stoic language because they were the main interlocutors. But are the Stoics also the source of the challenge to which this theory seems to be responding? The suggestion is attractive. It would fit a pattern of evolving and creative Aristotelian engagement with other schools of thought and point helpfully towards what some think is the most important contribution Aristotelian ethics can still make today: not a contribution to virtue theory in a narrow sense, but rather in the search for independently plausible naturalistic foundations for ethics.

We turn now to the topic of the passions and to what we can learn about Aristotelian ethics in this period from Cicero and from Seneca. We've said a good deal about Cicero already on other topics, but he also plays a major role in the topic of the passions. For most readers

Cicero's philosophical significance is probably more familiar than Seneca's, whose relationship to the various schools active in his day is a topic that still demands serious work and reflection. Perhaps the biggest gap in our understanding of Seneca is on the question of his relationship to the Peripatetics. Aristotelianism plays a role in Seneca's engagement with Greek philosophy that is perhaps less exciting than that of Platonism or the Cynics, certainly less familiar, but in my view no less significant. The Peripatetics are an important factor in Seneca's thoughts about the nature of the good, in his views on practical reason and deliberation, and most especially in his thinking about the passions.

As we consider what Seneca can tell us about the place of Aristotelians in the middle of the first century CE, it might be helpful to consider the catalogue of dead and dying schools of philosophy that he gives at the end of book 7 of the *Natural Questions* and that tells us so much about his view of the state of philosophy at Rome in the mid first century CE. Strikingly, the Peripatetics are *absent* from this list of moribund schools, as are the Platonists. The schools whose imminent demise Seneca laments include the Old and New Academies, Pyrrhonism, the Pythagoreans, and the followers of Sextius. The New Academy had died with Philo of Larisa in the first century BCE. Apparently the Antiochean Old Academy also failed to make it to the Augustan period in anything like full health. Pyrrhonism must refer to the sect founded by Aenesidemus in the mid first century BCE, in the aftermath of the blow-up in the Academy. How Seneca could have thought it moribund is something of a mystery, given the later flourishing of Pyrrhonism in the form of Sextus Empiricus. (Neo-)Pythagoreans flourished in the late first century BCE and beyond, so it is surprising to hear that they too are already moribund, though in this case the assessment seems right, at least for Rome. The Sextii, a short-lived and distinctively Roman school, are generally agreed to have been a mere flash in the pan.[26]

The philosophical sects that are *not* picked out as dead men walking are more important. Platonism of the dogmatic variety, based on a fuller use of the dialogues than Antiochus's revivalism had made; Stoicism, obviously; Epicureanism is also *not* picked out as being on the wane; and the Peripatetics. Plato plays a special role in Seneca's intellectual formation, and one of the most significant developments since Cicero's day and the post-Antiochean focus on commentary is that by now Platonism (rather than Academic skepticism) is fully and sharply distinguished from the Peripatetics. In the environment shaped by Antiochus's views, the Peripatetics and Academics stood together (along with the slightly suspect Stoics) in the big tent of the Old Academy. In Seneca, with Antiocheanism dead, Platonism is just as likely to be aligned with the Stoics against the Peripatetics—and certainly, Seneca sees Aristotelian philosophy as a movement to be vigorously resisted.

In considering the issue of Seneca's reaction to the Peripatetics on the subject of the passions, it is impossible to avoid the comparison with Cicero. For Cicero too, like Seneca, saw Stoic and Peripatetic theories of the passions as being fundamentally opposed. When presenting the Stoic theory of the passions in the *Tusculan Disputations,* Cicero found the foil he needed not in Plato but in the views developed in Aristotle's school during the Hellenistic period. Seneca took a similar view, broadly speaking, but with an important difference that readers have often sensed but have not, to my knowledge, put their finger on.[27]

For a long time it has been understood that the Hellenistic and early Imperial periods witnessed a dramatic increase in the attention paid to the *pathē* by philosophers. The passions were disciplined into a clear taxonomy by the Stoics, who emulated the categorization of the four cardinal virtues which seems to have been initiated by the influence of Plato's dialogues, especially the *Republic;* and they modeled their theory to some extent on the use of categorizations that Aristotle encouraged. The passions were defined, analyzed, and debated with a depth and sophistication that goes far beyond what one finds in any prior philosophical treatment. The Peripatetics followed the Stoic lead, as we can see from the treatise on the passions, *Peri Pathōn,* attributed erroneously to the Peripatetic Andronicus of Rhodes.[28] Throughout the Hellenistic period there had been, among Peripatetics, a marked shift with regard to the doctrine of the mean—the aim of a good person was no longer just to hit the mean in actions and passions but rather to attain *metriopatheia,* the Aristotelian counterpart to the Stoic ideal of *apatheia.* In fact, in the increasingly sharp debate between Peripatetics and Stoics which characterized ethics between the mid second century BCE and the first century CE, the passions became one of the two key points of debate (the other being the number and significance of the goods).[29]

At all the relevant periods, anger was the outstandingly important *pathos* and its centrality in discussions of the *pathē* increased as the Hellenistic period advanced. I should add here that grief, *lupē,* is the other highly salient passion in this period, a development stimulated no doubt by the often-cited work *On Grief* by the Academic Crantor (see, e.g., Cicero *Acad.* 2.135). Crantor also, according to Cicero, had positive things to say about anger, calling it the "whetstone of courage"—a very important forerunner of Peripatetic arguments later in the period.[30] As for anger, various treatises had been devoted to it, so that Seneca's *On Anger* fits into an established tradition. In Aristotle himself the passions, *pathē,* and anger as the centrally important passion, played an important role in two domains, in ethics and in rhetoric.[31] In the *Rhetoric* Aristotle gave his practically minded readers a lucid account of what anger is like, the role it plays in most people's lives, and a primer on how an orator can use it to get the reactions he wants from his audience. In the *Ethics* he has a few, a small few, remarks to make about anger and irascibility as features of our life that we must moderate if we are to live a solidly good life.

And that's about it. What we cannot readily find—and this is the important starting point for understanding what we see in Cicero and Seneca—is a commitment by Aristotle to the idea that anger is indispensable to our normal lives as a stimulus or motivation for morally significant actions. At the very most, I think, we can extract from the *Rhetoric* a weak version of the idea that the ability to provoke an audience to anger (something orators often need to do) is enhanced by a speaker's ability to project, as we would say, anger. This is a how-to tip for speakers of all sorts that Horace picks up when he says (and the point applies to anger as well as to sadness) "if you want me to weep you've got to grieve yourself": *si vis me flere, dolendum est primum ipsi tibi* (*Ars Poetica* 99 ff.). This is a point, a practical orator's point, that Cicero also makes both in his *Orator,* somewhat conversationally (128 ff.), and in the more didactic *De Oratore* (2.189 ff.). The ability to feign anger (or grief or any other passion) is an important tool in speaker's kit, just as it is for an actor, a teacher, perhaps even for parents from time to time.

Cicero's how-to tip for speakers is of limited theoretical significance, and it doesn't have much to do with philosophical reflection on the passions. It has its roots not just in common sense and widespread experience but also in the practical remarks made by Aristotle. Its presence in the tradition of rhetorical teaching hardly blunts its Peripatetic associations—if anything it emphasizes it; and this is just the sort of emotional manipulation that Stoic rhetoric stereotypically demands that we avoid. That considerations of this order reappear in the Stoic riposte to Peripatetic arguments is, then, all the more interesting.

It quickly becomes clear to any reader of Seneca's *On Anger* that the main opponents Seneca has in view are Aristotelians. Theophrastus and Aristotle are named, though it is very difficult to confirm that Seneca is actually referring to particular works or parts of works that we can identify. It is evident that the debate between schools on this issue did have a serious prehistory for Seneca, though the only really good glimpse we get of this debate comes in Cicero's *Tusculan Disputations*, book 4.[32]

In the Stoic classification which Seneca inherits, anger is classified as a type of desire (see, e.g., Cicero *TD* 4.21). It is, as Margaret Graver (2002) translates the passage:

> "desire to punish a person who is thought to have harmed one unjustly."
> Heatedness is "anger at its inception, when it has just come to be"; in
> Greek it is called *thumōsis*. Hatred is "inveterate anger." Rancor is "anger
> biding its time for revenge." Soreness of heart is "a more bitter anger
> which has its birth in the depths of mind and heart."

Both the definition of anger as a form of desire and the instant gravitation to lists of subtypes are characteristic of Stoicism;[33] indeed, they are abundantly paralleled in a range of texts, including Diogenes Laërtius (7.113) and Stobaeus (2.7, p. 91 Wachsmuth). Stoic priority is worth emphasizing here, since the slide into a list of subtypes is emulated by the Peripatetic list in pseudo-Andronicus:[34]

> *Thumos* is anger just beginning. *Cholos* is anger swelling up. *Pikria* is anger
> that breaks out instantly. *Mēnis* is anger stored up for a long time. *Kotos*
> is anger which watches for the best time for revenge. (*Peri Pathōn* ch. 4)

As the parallels given by Glibert-Thirry suggest,[35] the Peripatetic list was affected by some source that also lies behind Cicero's rather different catalogue—individual selection and adaptation by Cicero is as unsurprising as is his struggle with appropriate translation.

More important for our purposes is the discussion, later in book 4 of the *Tusculan Disputations,* of the *usefulness* of anger. Beginning in 4.38, Cicero directly opposes his Peripatetic opponents. He regards them as softies who try to accommodate the passions in our lives by putting a limit on them—a move which Stoics regard as wholly unrealistic, on the grounds that such a violent psychological phenomenon, once initiated, cannot be reliably curbed. It is worth pausing to note the change in dialectical framing here. For Aristotle, virtues are described in positive terms as mean states of action and passion; no serious attempt is made to define *pathē* for their own sake, let alone to give a fundamental justification for them. Their basic characteristics and their presence in our lives are taken for granted. Cicero, following the Stoics, begins from the assumption that passions are negative forces in life for which some justification is needed if we are to accept them as part of a morally successful life. And for this purpose the application of moderation is judged inadequate. Clearly there has been a reversal of onus in the debate, a major change from the state of affairs in Aristotle himself and his early followers.

The argument about the usefulness of anger begins in section 43 of book 4, and it is clear that Cicero, following the Stoics, presents the claim of usefulness as a counteroffensive by the Peripatetics—thus, it presupposes the reversal of onus I have noted. That this counteroffensive is distinctively Peripatetic is clear in Cicero. "They say not only that [the passions] are natural, but even that *nature gave them to us to serve some useful end.*" Here we see a characteristically Peripatetic invocation of natural teleology to justify a feature of or value in human life.[36]

It would be hard to prove definitively that Hellenistic Aristotelians actually invoked natural teleology in defense of anger and other passions as a positive element in human life, but they certainly continued and developed this feature of Aristotelian philosophy in other areas, and there is no particular reason to doubt that they did so here. Hence I am not at all suspicious of Cicero's claim that they regarded the passions as an endowment given by nature for a natural purpose—Cicero adds in 4.44 that the Peripatetics regarded other forms of desire too as having a natural function. The examples he adds are desire for recognition or approval (Themistocles and Demosthenes) and desire for knowledge (Pythagoras, Democritus, Plato). Even forms of pain *(lupē)* were regarded as useful (4.45–46). Shame, pity, jealousy, and resentment, even fear have all been given to us by nature for a purpose.

It is useful to keep in mind the dialectical situation that Cicero outlines. When forced to justify the passions in a way that the founders of their school had not been, Peripatetics respond by developing a new line of defense, but one that rests on typically Aristotelian natural teleology. Cicero's Stoic rebuttal of this defense similarly focuses on anger (4.48–55) but extends itself to include the other passions too (4.55–56), though much more briefly. Admittedly, for the most part Cicero's response does not directly address the claim about teleology; instead, he emphasizes the negative aspects of anger. To this the Peripatetics could reply that, as regrettable as such traits may be, they are still necessary to achieve nature's goals.[37] In response to the Peripatetic position, Cicero aims not to refute directly, but rather to undercut. He argues that anger is in fact redundant, that the features of human life which the Peripatetics allege require anger do not really require it. Hence he claims that courage, when properly understood, can perform its function without anger. This too is an important aspect of the claim that artificial anger suffices, that one need not be genuinely angry to get the job done. Cicero had hinted at this possibility when invoking the courage of Theseus (4.50—"indeed, it may well be that courage is not a matter of rage at all and that this anger of yours is a sham"), but Cicero's main emphasis (4.55) is on the very point that

Aristotle gestured at in the *Rhetoric*, that phony anger is as effective as the real thing *in swaying an audience*. And if phony anger serves the same end, there really is no need for the speaker to suffer the real thing with all its negative side effects.

Over all, the anti-Peripatetic argument in Cicero has a simple form. Since anger can be shown to be causally unnecessary, it is redundant and so justifies nothing. In a teleological context we can explain and justify a characteristic (even a negative trait) if it is hypothetically necessary to produce a desirable end. But if it is not in fact necessary, then the justification evaporates. So once the burden of justification had been shifted onto the Peripatetics and once they shouldered that burden by invoking a natural-teleological justification, the Stoic rebuttal came to focus almost entirely on whether anger really is in fact causally required for living a good life and behaving properly. If the job can get done in some other way and that other way of doing it does not have the negative impacts that anger and the other passions have, then natural teleology will prefer the solution which does not rely on anger.

That the debate in Cicero focusses on natural teleology is confirmed by his own concluding summary (4.79), which invokes utility and naturalness. From the Peripatetic point of view, it would perhaps have been better if the burden for justifying passions had not been shifted onto them, but by the first century BCE it was too late to worry about that. The best response to the demand for justification was to draw on the kind of natural teleology which all the Socratic schools agreed would be acceptable (after all, Chrysippus even accepted that bedbugs were a justifiable feature of the natural world because their bites were needed to get us out of bed in the morning[38]). And to that the Stoic response, as we see it in Cicero, was simple and direct: anger is a massively negative feature of human life and would only be justifiable if it were absolutely necessary for the carrying out of unmistakably good ends. The Peripatetics claim that it is necessary for certain vital functions, but in fact it is not. We can, say the Stoics, get the job done otherwise. So in a rational and orderly world there is in fact no justification for the passions; they are redundant and have no role to play in a good human life. Cicero gives us a smoothly rhetorical version of one side of a very real philosophical debate.

But what of the argument in Seneca? The *De Ira* is long, a rich and complex work. So I can only deal with a small portion of it. Given the prominence of the preexisting debate between Stoics and Peripatetics on this issue, it is only fitting and not at all surprising that at the beginning of the work, shortly after giving a Stoic definition of anger,[39] Seneca adduces a version of Aristotle's definition from the *De Anima* (I.3). Not only is this the only other definition credited to a specific school, but Seneca introduces it by saying "Aristotle's definition is not far from ours."[40] Thus the stage is set for a debate between Peripatetics and Stoics. After a brief dismissal of the multitude of subtypes of anger—he is much less tolerant than Cicero of this kind of *technologia*—Seneca tackles the central Peripatetic justification of anger as we know it from Cicero's account: is anger natural (I.5)? Cicero's Peripatetics had claimed that anger is a *gift from nature*, given for a clear purpose. Here, Seneca merely considers whether anger is *secundum naturam*, whether it coheres with human nature (it doesn't; see especially I.6.4). Dispensing moral criticism (*castigatio*), he adds, does not require anger (I.6), no matter what his opponents say. And those opponents are pretty clearly Peripatetic—Seneca wields the club of *modus*, the mean, in his refutation of them and invokes the authority of Plato (I.6.5), thus lining up the authoritative godfather of the Socratic family against the upstart Aristotelians. Here is further confirmation that the Antiochean construction of one big happy Old Academic family is long gone.

Seneca then invokes the argument, familiar as Peripatetic from Cicero, in I.7.I. "Can it really be that anger, although it is not natural, should be adopted because it has often proved useful? It rouses and spurs on the mind. Without it, courage can achieve nothing magnificent in war—without the flame of anger beneath, to goad men on to meet danger with boldness." Though the "whetstone of courage" argument goes back ultimately to the Academic Crantor and to popular opinion, in context it is presented as a Peripatetic move. Seneca responds by noting that some people want, therefore, to moderate rather than eliminate anger (a view already marked as non-Platonic); it is this claim that anger is subject to moderation that he challenges in his rebuttal. In I.9.I Seneca generalizes and claims that there is *nothing* useful in anger. Apparently the "whetstone of courage" claim was the Peripatetics' best effort. In I.9.2 Seneca even attributes a vivid little speech to Aristotle himself—given Seneca's habits of *prosopopoiia*, it cannot be thought of as a purported quotation from the master and need not even be taken for the words of any later Peripatetic.

> Anger, says Aristotle, is needful; no fight can be won without it, without its filling the mind and kindling enthusiasm there; it must be treated, however, not as a commander but as one of the rank and file.

This, Seneca continues to argue, is false. And the argument again turns on the pointed anti-Peripatetic claim that no *modus* is possible with a passion like anger. There follows a lengthy, typically and splendidly Senecan elaboration of this general point. High points in the rant are the rebuttal of the imagined argument (I.12) that anger is appropriate and indeed necessary if one is to defend one's father and mother from murder and rape respectively. The Stoic rejoinder is simple. Doing the right thing, filial devotion, etc., are sufficient motivations. Why, then, mess with excess? Anger involves risks and negative side effects.

Why bother if there is no need? At I.12.3 we have another invocation, probably imaginative and rhetorical again, this time of Theophrastus.

> Good men are angry at wrongs done to their friends. When you say this, Theophrastus, you cast odium on braver teachings. You turn from the judge to the gallery.

—that is, you rely on popular opinion rather than the discerning *sententia* of experts. Theophrastus is again criticized at I.14.I:

> A good man, says Theophrastus, cannot help being angry at bad people.

The way this point is put marks anger as sign of weakness (he cannot help himself). It looks very much as though Seneca is here attacking a straw man.

The anti-Peripatetic theme continues at I.17.I, where Aristotle is brought back for a drubbing similar to the last one (and we should not forget that even in the therapeutic part of the *De Ira*, at 3.3.I, Aristotle is reprised for one final refutation), and at I.19.3, when dealing with the suggestion that anger might be justified because it is needed in punishment, one of his own followers, Hieronymus of Rhodes, is invoked against him.

> When you wish to hit someone, says Hieronymus, what need is there to bite your lips first?

Cooper and Procopé (1995 p. 37) take this physical gesture as an indication of repression, that Hieronymus is arguing *against* holding back one's anger. But the context and the metaphor suggest just the opposite, and that this is Seneca turning the Peripatetics against themselves (just as he turned Plato against them earlier and will do so again at I.19.7).[41] Book I ends with the height of anti-Peripatetic innuendo—anger cannot be justified by connecting it to *magnitudo animi, megalopsuchia,* a characteristically Aristotelian virtue.

What is striking in all of this, to my mind, is the absence of the argument from natural teleology that stood out so sharply in Cicero's treatment of this theme. Components of it are here. There is the argument that anger is incompatible with human nature, and even a focus on the costly trade-offs that in other contexts indicate an awareness of hypothetical necessity. (At 1.12.6 Seneca argues that some bad things are occasionally useful, such as fevers, shipwrecks, and so on. Regrettable, but necessary for a good outcome—just what one might expect a Peripatetic to say if he were wielding the argument that Cicero cites and rebuts.) But in Seneca we do not have the Peripatetic arguing from natural teleology and the Stoic replying to this argument. The dialectic in Seneca's text is quite different from that in Cicero's.

In book 2 Seneca twice brings in a point that Cicero acknowledges and that even has its roots in Aristotle's texts (as much of the other Peripatetic argument does not). Anger, Seneca says, may be needed for the sake of stirring up an audience—but then a speaker's pretense is all one really needs. "It may sometimes be simulated if the sluggish minds of the *audience* are to be aroused . . ." (2.14). And at the end of the dialectical part of the work (2.17) Seneca restates this point. "An orator is sometimes better for being angry. No, for *pretending* to be angry." He also deploys the whetstone argument one last time.

> Sluggish is the mind that lacks anger. True, if it has nothing stronger than anger. But one should not be the robber any more than the prey; one should neither be pitying nor cruel. The one state of mind is too soft, the other too hard. The wise man ought to strike a mean, approaching whatever calls for firm action, not with anger but with strength.

Again, Seneca turns the tables on the Peripatetics. The mean, it turns out, is *apatheia* rather than *metriopatheia*.[42]

Let me now take stock of what we might learn not about Stoicism itself but about the Aristotelian theories of the passions to which Cicero and Seneca respond so vigorously, on behalf of Stoicism. Given the differences between the *Tusculans* and the *De Ira* and indeed given the differences between Cicero and Seneca as authors, it is not surprising that the tenor of the dialectic in the two works should be so different. But it's not just that they dress up their anti-Peripatetic arguments in different clothing—with Seneca much readier to make *ad hominem* points by using their own concepts against his opponents. It may also be that Cicero and Seneca differ in their appreciation of the theory they are attacking. Cicero manifestly understands the role of natural teleology in the Peripatetic justification of anger—just as he appreciates and elaborates on the role of natural teleology in their general moral theory when he expounds a version of it in *On Goals* 5. Seneca, though he is working with very similar argumentative materials and even though he invokes "nature" in his critique, shows no interest at all in the natural teleology that underlies the Peripatetic theory as Cicero sees it. Seneca is only interested in a small, dialectical aspect of that theory, the "whetstone argument" taken on its own. Just possibly this difference should be laid exclusively at the doors of Cicero and Seneca, but I would like to suggest that that their respective targets are in fact different versions of Peripatetic theory on the passions. We have seen enough variety among Aristotelians to make this plausible, and there was no canonical text of the master to appeal to in imposing a standard Peripatetic approach.

Aristotelian ethics after Aristotle had embraced the notion, which was probably folk wisdom but certainly deployed by Crantor, that anger was needed as a motivational spur, as a stimulus for various kinds of good and necessary actions. Stoics were determined to combat this notion, which they believed to be deeply misguided, but Seneca and Cicero (when speaking on behalf of Stoics) did so in very different ways. Cicero tackled the problem at a significantly deeper level. Seneca was less concerned with the philosophical underpinnings of his opponents' position and let fly with dialectical and rhetorical counterargument—and little more. Since Seneca was more than able to take on serious philosophical argument at a serious philosophical level, one might wonder why he didn't in this case. It's not plausible any longer to explain this kind of shallowness by invoking his philosophical limitations.[43] I rather think—in fact, this is my concluding suggestion—that the reason for his style of argument should be sought in his opponents. If the Peripatetics Seneca was reacting to were less than profound, then he would happily meet them on their own level. He would rise, or sink, to the level of his interlocutors.

If we look at the differences between Cicero's and Seneca's critique in this light, then we can learn a good deal about Aristotelian theories of the passions from this brief analysis. We confirm, first of all, that later Aristotelian theories of the passions, especially anger, really are different from those of Aristotle himself. We learn that Aristotelians were content to adopt a line of argument drawn from both folk psychology and the Academic Crantor. And we learn as well that the Aristotelian theories against which Cicero (in the first century BCE) and Seneca (a century later) argued were in all likelihood significantly different from each other. Whichever Aristotelian theory Cicero attacked had a strong version of natural teleology built into its core. And the Aristotelian theory attacked by Seneca did not. This need not be taken as a sign of a linear development in the school's doctrines, but it ought, in my view, to be accepted as yet one more indication, if any were needed, of the variety among Aristotelian ethical theories in the ancient world.

Seneca didn't just criticize Aristotelian ethics for its position on the passions. He also treated them (and not Platonists) as his main opponents in the ongoing debate about the sufficiency of virtue for happiness. This was a dominant theme in the second half of Cicero's *On Goals*, where the opponents of the hardline Stoic position were the Old Academics of Antiochus, but in *Letter* 85 it is Peripatetics who are the representatives of the anti-Stoic position on this topic. Here the opponents are explicitly named; the same is true in *Letter* 87, where the argument against the Peripatetics centers on the nature of the good. In this letter the commitment of Aristotelians to the *tria genera bonorum* is highlighted,[44] and Seneca devotes considerable dialectical resources (including Aristotelian-style syllogisms) to refuting their position. I don't have room for a detailed analysis of these arguments here,[45] and I should emphasize that these letters do not exhaust Seneca's polemical engagement with Aristotelian ethics. Let me instead pause to reflect briefly on the big picture. Seneca is a Roman, a nonprofessional philosopher, writing for Roman readers in the middle of the first century CE; we have no reason to doubt him when he presents himself as continuing to attend philosophical "schools" well into old age (see the opening of *Letter* 76), so he is presumably *au fait* with philosophical life in Rome, which by his day had become one of the two or three main centers of activity in the Empire. For Seneca, and presumably for many of his peers, Aristotelian ethics stands out as a highly influential, perhaps even a dominant voice in contemporary debate. We don't know the names of any important contemporary Aristotelians, but they must have been active and must have had an audience. And their work was not commentary or paraphrase; it was not presented as a reconstruction of the philosophy of the old masters, as the Antiochean Old Academy was.

I think this is pretty good evidence that Aristotelian ethics was thriving in the middle of the first century CE and that it was still a creative force, engaging dialectically with other schools, not just developing commentaries on Aristotle's works. This suggestion fits well, I think, with what we might conclude from reflection on Harry's little treatise and from some of what we know about the influence of Aristotelian ethical in the later first century CE. For Plutarch and Epictetus both show signs of responding to Aristotelianism. The latter famously adopted and reused Aristotle's signature technical term, *prohairesis*, for his own renewed version of Stoic moral theory; and in his essay *On Moral Virtue*, Plutarch made strikingly creative use of the Aristotelian concepts form and matter in working out a fresh theory of the passions, one that he hoped would give to Platonism new resources against Stoic opponents. And it succeeded in that goal, as is widely acknowledged. It is perhaps not so often noticed that coopting Aristotelian theory in the development of one's own is also a highly effective strategy against Aristotelians themselves.

We probably cannot know whether Plutarch, like Alcinous, drew more on Aristotle's ethical treatises or on contemporary Aristotelian philosophers with whom debates and discussions were ongoing. But we can be reasonably confident that both elements were in play. Seneca's works, Harry's little treatise, the scraps of information preserved from later antiquity (including from Alexander) about the range of Aristotelian theories known from this period—all of this establishes that the tradition of lively and innovative Aristotelian ethics carried on well into the early empire, even as the commentary tradition, destined for ultimate victory, gathered momentum.

5

Alexander and Imperial Aristotelianism

I have argued that innovative approaches to Aristotelian ethics continued to be significant well into the first century of the Roman Empire, and that they weren't limited to the growth of the commentary tradition. After Xenarchus, in the late first century BCE we met the occasionally somewhat awkward but definitely creative developments in the work of "Harry," the author of Doxography C. Some Peripatetic put together a treatise on the passions which was deeply influenced by Stoic definitions and adapted them to Aristotelian ends—a work which came to be attributed to Andronicus of Rhodes. And this is also the probable date of a little work *On Virtues and Vices*, not a very profound work but one which, like the cosmological treatise *On the Cosmos*, made its way into the *corpus Aristotelicum* itself. So it is not implausible to suggest that Seneca's Peripatetic opponents, who seem to be just as creative as any of these other Aristotelians, were real, contemporary philosophers, either working in Rome or possibly merely influential there in the middle of the first century CE. We will see later in this chapter that Alexander of Aphrodisias provides further evidence of creative work by Aristotelian philosophers that is not part of the commentary tradition represented by Aspasius: Sosicrates and a Roman philosopher, Verginius Rufus, advanced positions on the naturalistic foundations of ethics which Alexander himself had to take seriously. These philosophers cannot be dated with confidence, but it is suggestive that the only known candidate for the identity of our Roman Aristotelian is an aristocrat mentioned by Tacitus.

If Aristotelian ethics is a creative, going concern in the late first century, then it is not at all surprising that the Platonist Plutarch found it natural to adopt Aristotelian doctrine in his own development of Platonic ethics. His little treatise *On Moral Virtue*, more often studied in recent years for what it says about Stoic moral psychology than for its own positive doctrines, is a clear indication of the continuing influence of Aristotelian ethics in the larger philosophical arena. Plutarch begins (440d) from the sharp contrast between reason and passion that we have come to see as typical of Hellenistic Aristotelianism and pays tribute to the characteristic doctrines of that school by aligning reason, in moral psychology, with form *(eidos)* and passion with matter *(hulē)*. The passions are, as it were, raw material for the creative power of our reason to work on. This is an application of Aristotelian doctrine that clearly suggests a completely immanent, hylomorphic conception of human nature; human reason is, on this account, inextricably bound up in its relationship with the body and its passions.[1] That, of course, is a conclusion which Plutarch as a Platonist finds somewhat disconcerting, so he asserts somewhat abruptly (440de) and without argument that "I think it's obvious that virtue can also come into being and persist as something free of matter and unmixed."[2] And then he moves on to a general survey of his predecessors.

In the course of this survey Plato's views are of course highlighted, and Aristotle is portrayed (442bc) as having begun from his teacher's position and then subsequently revised his views, moving from tripartition to bipartition of the soul. Throughout, it is clear that Plutarch is familiar with the works of Aristotle, that he has in mind the treatises and not just the views of contemporaries who claim to speak for Aristotle. But the influence of Aristotelianism goes beyond the doxographical review. For Plutarch it is completely natural to treat virtue as a mean state, and in chapter 6, without allusion to Aristotle, he blends this doctrine with a typically Platonist application of harmonic theory. And in his lengthy discussion of self-control and its failure, the influence of Aristotle's analysis is unmistakable.

Plutarch's arguments are for the most part directed against the Stoics, who are spoken of in the present tense as his dialectical adversaries although their views are defined by the positions taken by Zeno and Chrysippus—this is why the treatise has been so important as evidence for Hellenistic Stoicism. Aristotelian ethics is enlisted as an ally in this debate. Plutarch deploys the doctrines of Aristotle's ethical treatises constructively and creatively, but he also uses in his own voice, without allusion to those treatises, some paradigmatically Aristotelian ideas, such as the doctrine of the mean and the contrast of form and matter. Since we have indications from elsewhere that Aristotelians continued to participate in debate and to generate new developments of Aristotelian ethics, it seems reasonable to regard Plutarch's work as further confirmation that the philosophical scene continued to embrace fresh contributions from the heirs of Aristotle.

In the decades between Plutarch and Aspasius, whose commentary on Aristotle's *Ethics* marks a turning point in the school's history, other evidence from the Platonist side reinforces this general picture.

For example, in his handbook, Alcinous,[3] in chapters 20–30 and 32 on the virtues and the passions, shows an openness to Aristotelian positions that resembles what we see in Plutarch, though strikingly he avoids Aristotelian approaches to other topics quite firmly. This is unsurprising if Aristotelian philosophers, especially those interested in ethics, are in active dialogue with Platonists at the time. Of course, not all Platonists could accept this kind of influence. The roughly contemporary Atticus, for example, is magnificently eloquent on the need to keep Platonism pure of contamination from other schools. But even this rejection, I think, is evidence of contemporary activity by Aristotelians. Why rail against a nonexistent enemy?

But it is one thing to infer from their opponents that Aristotelians were still a force to be reckoned with, and quite another to be able to identify individuals or their particular contributions. For the most part, sadly, the second century CE gives us little. Aspasius, of course, is a commentator, and my particular interest is in the noncommentary tradition. So at this point we come finally to the greatest Aristotelian of the Roman Imperial era, Alexander of Aphrodisias. Though he too is known best for his commentaries, he is for my purposes even more important as a philosophical essayist. And it is on that aspect of his work that I intend to focus.

Alexander[4] was a philosopher "imperial" in many ways, not just in date: from his magisterial dominance over his school's tradition, to his bold ambition of forging a unified body of doctrine out of the often discordant strains of Aristotle's various works—this was, no doubt, in emulation of the great movements in contemporary Platonism—to the simple fact that he enjoyed a privileged career as the occupant of a chair funded by the Imperial purse. What we know of his work outside the commentaries is considerable. We still possess his great anti-Stoic treatise addressed to the emperors, on the topic of fate, in which he grapples not just with Stoicism of the Hellenistic era but also with more contemporary opponents, such as Philopator.[5] He also argued against Stoic physics in a lengthy treatise *On Mixture*.[6] He wrote an independent treatise *On the Soul*,[7] and there survive important collections of essays from Alexander and his school. One is preserved as a kind of appendix to the book on the soul[8] and the others come to us organized as four books of "problems."[9] Alexander was so prolific that there is space only to touch the surface of his work, choosing one or two themes for discussion which will connect to some of the more important issues raised in earlier chapters, and in particular the theme of ethical naturalism.

In doing so, I will be zeroing in on a small but critically important section of Alexander's appendix to his treatise on the soul (*Mantissa* pp. 150–153) and to a shorter stretch of essay 1 in his *Ethical Problems*. For at least in these two places we find Alexander taking the basic insights of Aristotelian naturalism, the idea that human beings, like the rest of nature, are naturally disposed to strive for being, in the sense of being active or actual rather than passive or potential, and applying those principles to issues that are essential to moral philosophy. In doing this he expresses himself in a language of nature and natural attachments drawn from the post-Aristotelian world. Although Aristotle's own works sometimes anticipate such terminology, the closest relevant antecedents for his analysis can be found in the philosophers Alexander discusses here and, we should recall, in the work of Harry (Doxography C) and in book 5 of Cicero's *On Goals*.

We look first, and briefly, at the first essay in the collection we now know as the *Ethical Problems*. Here Alexander raises "difficulties against those who say that life is not a good." These opponents are clearly Stoics, for whom being alive is *not* indeed a good, but merely a preferred indifferent.[10] This distinction was quite important for the Stoics, since it preserved the incommensurable value of virtue and permitted them to explain how prerational humans could be motivated by a desire for self-preservation (that is, staying alive) that nevertheless would yield to a motivation to pursue the genuine good once reason was achieved.

But the Stoic position was, not unreasonably, seen as less attuned to what is natural than it should be—and this was in spite of their claim to follow nature; the nature followed is altogether too cosmic and theological to pass muster and their developmental story involved positing an unconfirmable and suspect alteration in human nature at the point when reason is acquired. Aristotelians, by contrast, as we saw even in Piso's theory, maintained that the principles which govern natural entities, animal or plant, were fully immanent (not relying on cosmic teleology), the same for all animals of all species, continuously throughout their lives. The drive to *be* what one is, as Harry put it, could be invoked as a natural principle in all contexts. And in Aristotle's view, to be is to be *actual* or active, ultimately to do what one's nature gives one the potential for.[11] And this meant that the universal principle of natural philosophy (that potential strives to be actual) also turns out to be a principle invoked in ethics. Alexander took the same line, but he is much more deeply involved than his predecessors were in connecting this with the exegesis of Aristotle's own texts.

In *Problem* I (118.23–120.2) Alexander avoids taking an easy way out. Stoics deny that life is a good, but they agree that it is a preferred indifferent. Critolaus, Antiochus, and others dealt with this as a mere verbal distinction: the Stoics are just being "word warriors" again; what they really mean is that life is a good, but they are too stubborn to use that special term; hence they really hold the same doctrine but pretend to be innovators. That response would be too easy, papering over the real differences between Stoics and Aristotelians.

Instead, Alexander invokes a teleological principle: when there is a potentiality for opposites, the opposites for which it is a potentiality are not related to it symmetrically. Each potentiality "has as its goal the *better* of the things for which it is a potentiality; where there is potentiality, the worse [outcome] comes about through some mischance" (118.27). This is a principle that we see operating in the crafts (navigation, carpentry, etc.) and (true to his Aristotelian principles) Alexander applies the principle as we see it in the crafts, where it is relatively clear, to the more debatable state of affairs in nature. "And as it is with the things that are brought about by craft, so it is in the case of those that come about by nature" (119.4–5). As we might say, we can tell that nature is biased towards the good because we see the same situation in the crafts and we are presumed already to know (from reading Aristotle, I guess) that the crafts are particularly reliable in giving us a window onto nature.[12] Both Aristotle and later Peripatetics held that there could be no more natural drive than the desire to exist, to develop into full actuality (which is equivalent to complete being), and the Stoics would have considerable difficulty in denying this drive at least as a starting point for ethics—since their foundations of ethics were built on the doctrine of *oikeiōsis* which maintains that our basic drive is to preserve oneself. Hence it was natural that Alexander should adopt what he regarded as a shared doctrine in this essay. Here is the relevant passage (119.18–30), in Sharples's (1990a) translation, with minor changes:

> Life, too, has in itself the potentiality for living either well or badly, and is given to us by nature with a view to our living well. For it is not possible for us to possess [the actuality of living well] as soon as we come into existence; there is nothing perfect in what is incomplete, and

everything is incomplete immediately after it comes into existence. [It follows, then, that life too] will be a thing to be valued with a view to the *best* of the things that can come about in us. For what is best, and the end [at which we aim], is living well, and this cannot come about with life [itself]. How is it not inconsistent to say that [life] is something to which we are attached [Sharples translates this as "endeared," *oikeiōsthai*] by nature, and that we do everything with a view to our own preservation, and simultaneously to deny that nature attaches us to it as a *good?* That we are attached to life as a good is clear both from [our] being very concerned about producing children, on the grounds that we will in a way exist in future through them, and also through [our] fearing everything we fear [all] the more because we are apprehensive that it will cause our death.

The echoes of book 9 of the *Nicomachean* and book 7 of the *Eudemian Ethics* are unmistakable.[13] So are the allusions to and jabs at Stoic theory. What brings it all together for Alexander, though, is a basic teleological principle of great scope, applied to a problem in ethics. That "things which are intermediate are judged on the basis of their potentiality for what is better" (119.30) is a principle in physics as well as ethics, and Alexander is aware of the persuasive power that flows from such generality.

The other essay which tackles similar naturalistic foundations for ethics is in the so-called *Mantissa* of Alexander's treatise *On the Soul*.[14] It is moderate in length, just over three pages in the Berlin Academy edition (Supp. 2.1, pp. 150–153),[15] and bears the title "The Aristotelians' [views] on the primary object of attachment." Despite its length, this is such an important text for my topic that I include here a full translation of my own (though readers will naturally want to consult Sharples 2004 as well, as it includes very helpful notes).

112

The Views of the Aristotelians about
the Primary Object of Attachment
Alexander (*Mantissa* pp. 150–153)

Since there is an object of desire and a faculty of desire, and since there
is also an ultimate object of desire, viz. happiness, and since what is
ultimate is ultimate relative to something primary, there will also be a
primary object of desire. For indeed, wherever there is an ultimate on a
continuum, there must also be on that continuum a starting point from
which there is a progression through intermediates to the end and ultimate point. Consequently, if there is an ultimate object of desire there
is a starting point relative to it, and that is what they call the primary
object of attachment [*prōton oikeion*]. And this is the "primary object
of attachment" whose identification has been the subject of enquiry
by philosophers. The views of philosophers on this have differed, but
generally speaking, those who take a position on it hold that the distinguishing feature of the primary object of desire corresponds to the
distinguishing feature of the ultimate object of desire.

At any rate, the Stoics, though not all of them, say that the animal is the primary object of attachment for itself (for each animal
is attached to itself as soon as it is born and this definitely includes
human beings); but those Stoics who are thought to speak with more
sophistication and to make more articulations about it say that as
soon as we are born we are attached to our constitution and to the
preservation of ourselves. The Epicureans held that the primary object
of attachment is pleasure without qualification and they say that as
we mature this pleasure is articulated. Others, such as the Megarians,
held that it is freedom from upset, while the Academics held that it is
avoidance of precipitate errors. For they say that our primary attachment is to this, so that we won't stumble at any point. And in general,

as we said, each group supposes that the starting points correspond to the final objects of desire.

Some say that, according to Aristotle, the primary object of attachment is ourselves. For if the object of love is an object of desire (in fact, we do not love anyone more than ourselves nor are we attached to anything else in this way; for indeed we strive for other things and love certain other things in virtue of a reference to ourselves), then each person would in this regard be the primary object of attachment for himself. Xenarchus and Boethus were of this opinion, basing their view on what is said about friendship in book 8 of the *Nicomachean Ethics* (1155b17–26); and in book 9 he says something similar (1168a35–b10).[16] But this view is unarticulated. For we love ourselves either (a) on the grounds that we are *objects* of desire, like some wholly distinct thing, separate from ourselves, that we desire (since nothing desires itself nor does it desire what it already has in so far as it has it); or (b) we desire that we ourselves should *be* without qualification, since the other way [of desiring ourselves] is impossible (for we are not distinct from ourselves). Therefore [we would desire to exist] even in a wretched and painful condition; for even in those circumstances we still *are.*

Others say that, according to Aristotle, the primary object of attachment is pleasure; they too are inspired by what he says in the *Nicomachean Ethics.*[17] For he says that there are three objects of desire: the fine, the advantageous, and the pleasant. And an object of desire is something to which we have an attachment. But we come to grasp the noble and the advantageous as we get older, but we grasp the pleasant immediately. So if these are the only objects of desire and attachment, and if the first of these is the pleasant, then this would be the primary object of attachment. Again, if all desire is for the good or the apparent good, but the genuine good is final while the apparent good is not like this, and if the pleasant is an apparent good, then this would be our primary natural object of desire. This too is an unarticulated account. For we desire what is pleasant in order to acquire it for ourselves, though we do not have an unqualified relationship of attachment to it; [we desire] either what is pleasant without qualification or what is pleasant in some manner (i.e., is pleasant in some respect).[18]

Verginius Rufus and before him Sosicrates[19] said that each person desires perfection [*teleiotēs*], i.e., being in activity, obviously being active with no impediment. That is why he says that for us too being in activity is an object of desire, and this is being alive and the activities dependent on life, which are pleasant. For this kind of natural activity is, as long as it is unimpeded, pleasant. But for each thing its perfection is a good. And for everything that is potential, its perfection is to become in activity what it was potentially, and animals exist not in virtue of being in activity but in virtue of being potential (for in fact we are alive while sleeping). Therefore, by desiring to be in activity, one would desire one's own proper [*oikeias*] perfection. And this is a good for each, so that we desire it. It is consistent for those who postulate that the primary object of attachment is being and living in activity to say that the primary object of attachment and the good is pleasure. Moreover, the end [*telos*] is in harmony with this. For the end is being active with regard to intellect and for the object of intellection[20] to be in actuality, and this depends on our having an attachment to what is potentially so. When a human being becomes mature he has a being which consists in being intellectual.

This account is in need of articulation and a distinction: as soon as we are born, do we desire *every* activity dependent on life (these being pleasant) or not every one? For perhaps we do not desire the best one, since this is final and ultimate. Or is their claim that we desire that activity corresponding to what we *are* and at that point we are perceptual (so that we desire the activity of the senses) and later on we are rational? In book 10 of the *Nicomachean Ethics* [1176b26] Aristotle says, "for each person the activity in accord with its proper condition is most choiceworthy."

These are the views about the primary object of attachment according to the Peripatetics. But the topic is in need of more careful articulation. For since, as Aristotle says, the end is twofold (in one sense it is *what* it is and in the other it is *who it is for*), the "what" is happiness (for this is the ultimate and greatest of all goods and is the goal [aimed at]) and the "who it is for" is *us* (for the most final [i.e, endlike] thing for us is for us to acquire happiness), and as regards objects, happiness is the end and goal, and as regards us, it is us being happy. So since the end is twofold, there must also be a kind of duality in the starting points, with each starting point leading to its proper end by way of the continuity of the objects of desire. Therefore, as we say, the primary object of desire too is compound. For not only are we most attached to ourselves, but as well we are not attached to ourselves without qualification, but rather with an eye to acquiring good things for ourselves. So this primary object of attachment is our good and we desire this. Since it is impossible to obtain a grasp of the genuine good as soon as we are born, we desire the apparent good. And the pleasant is the apparent good. Therefore what is pleasant for us is our primary object of attachment, i.e., the apparent good. And even if it is consistent for others who say that this is the first object of attachment because their theories must be internally consistent, nevertheless, since *they* have not made divisions and distinctions, some of them say that the primary object of attachment is us, and others say that it is the external pleasant object; but none of them put the two aspects together and finished the whole theory. At any rate, both groups taken together make a sound claim while each taken separately makes an unsound claim.

Or rather, the articulated account is the one given by him who says that the object of attachment for each is being in activity and living[21] continuously in accordance with the essence of [lit: being for] each (for what accords with nature, in so far as it is the essence of each, is pleasant and an object of attachment and a primary object of desire). For a child, because he is not yet rational, would not be primarily attached to activity in accordance with being rational, but, since he is perceptual, he would be attached to the activities of the perceptual capacities and also to being nourished. In desiring unimpeded activity corresponding to what they are, they would desire their own proper [*oikeion*] good and pleasure—if, in fact, pleasure is the unimpeded activity of a natural state—and moreover would desire to acquire that activity for themselves (for they desire their own distinctive activity). For he who desires his own proper activity in accordance with what he is in potentiality obviously desires it in an unimpeded form (for what prevents and impedes an activity should be avoided by one who desires it); and at the same time this kind of activity is also pleasant. And he does not desire activity without qualification, but desires to be active itself[22] and desires his own proper activity; and the more so since pleasure is consequent upon the sort of activity to which it is primarily attached. For he hasn't made pleasure the goal of his desire, but has it as a consequence of the activity. For everything that is in accord with nature is pleasant.

For it is not as though he is first pleased and then as a result comes to desire that through which he was pleased. For nature is not in need of its own distinct reasoning [*oikeios logos*] but rather, for natural entities without exception a starting point of this kind [i.e., natural] is followed by its consequences and by an end of the same kind, providing that there is no impediment, the end not being the result of planning as in the case of the crafts, but rather just being built that way. The end as Aristotle states it (that is, activity according to virtue) is in harmony with this kind of starting point. Aristotle too says as follows in book 10 of the *Nicomachean Ethics*,[23] "One might well think that all humans desire pleasure because all of them also strive to be alive. Life is an activity and each person is active in relation to the objects and with the faculties that he likes best.[24] And pleasure completes those activities, as it also completes being alive, which they desire. So it is reasonable that they strive for pleasure. For it completes being alive for each human being, and this is precisely what is worth choosing."

This compact and elegant little essay has more often been mined for the information it provides about other schools (see SVF 3.183) than for the interest of its own argument; for it begins with what *appears* to be a neutral account of different schools' views on what the primary object of attachment is—the *prōton oikeion.* But Alexander's account is in fact far from neutral. It begins by presupposing as a conceptual framework two basic principles which are anything but self-evident, and it concludes by arguing that when one understands things properly each of the main competing theories is *half* right; only by putting the half-rights together do we see that Aristotle's theory (unsurprisingly) is the only one that proves to be fully adequate. What are these initial assumptions?

One is familiar from Cicero's *On Goals* and almost certainly has its origins in the critical and dialectical survey of Carneades.[25] As we learn from Cicero, in organizing all possible theories of the end *(telos)* Carneades held that the initial and precultural motivational condition of all animals had to be in close alignment with their *telos*— what we might dub the "alignment condition"[26]—not so called by Gisela Striker, though she has acutely directed our attention to it. Alexander announces at the beginning of his essay that "the views of philosophers on this have differed, but generally speaking those who take a position on it hold that the distinguishing feature of the *primary* object of desire corresponds to the distinguishing feature of the *ultimate* object of desire" (150.27–28). He soon (151.2–3) repeats the point: "And in general, as we said, each group supposes that the starting points correspond to the final objects of desire." This proves to be an effective tool to wield against both Epicureans and Stoics. For Epicureans start out with pleasure, which proves to be an embarrassment when linked to the adult motivations that are supposed to go with virtuous behavior—virtue gets reduced to a merely instrumental status. And the Stoics, he shows, need to postulate a discontinuity in moral motivation in order to get an intrinsic commitment to virtue out of a starting point that consists of a commitment to self-preservation. We have seen Antiochus and Piso struggle with this; Alexander will turn the alignment condition to his own advantage. For after reviewing the other schools' views and also the earlier attempts by various Peripatetics (none of which are "articulated" enough to meet Alexander's exacting standards), he makes an Aristotelian fresh start (152.15–24):

These are the views about the primary object of attachment according to the Peripatetics. But the topic is in need of more careful articulation. For since, as Aristotle says, the end is twofold (in one sense it is *what* it is and in the other it is *who it is for*), the "what" is happiness (for this is the ultimate and greatest of all goods and is the goal [aimed at]) and the "who it is for" is *us* (for the most final [i.e, end-like] thing for us is for us to acquire happiness); as regards objects happiness is the end and goal and as regards us it is us being happy. So since the end is twofold there must also be a kind of duality in the starting points, with each starting point leading to its proper end by way of the continuity of the objects of desire.

Alexander goes on to show how, when properly understood, the alignment condition is met only by Aristotle's theory. The duality associated here with final causation runs consistently right through the life of the human animal; it is not the kind of duality which involves a break between an early stage in which universally shared animal desires are the only motivations and a later stage where something distinctly and almost magically rational comes into play. Rather, it is a duality of aspects or senses. There are two aspects of the *telos* (the object aimed at as a goal and the beneficiary of the *telos* when the state is achieved).[27] And these two aspects correlate with the state of affairs in the newborn animal as well.

The second basic assumption is even more important to Alexander's argument. Like Piso and Harry, but in a manner systematically rooted in Aristotle's texts, Alexander assumes a uniform view about how animals function in the world. An animal is a living thing, and so it is alive by virtue of having capacities or potentials. The whole point of having potentials is to activate or actualize them, and doing so is the goal or end. Typically each potential and corresponding activity has a correlated object which is the required target for its fulfillment. These are absolutely general features of the natural world. From the beginning of the essay to its end, this Aristotelian principle of natural philosophy (most elaborately laid out in the *De Anima* but ubiquitous where relevant in Aristotle) structures Alexander's argument. Hence we focus not just on the object of desire *(orekton)* but also on the desiderative capacity in an animal *(orektikon)* (150.20); similarly, human nature is fulfilled when our capacity as thinkers and the capacity of the objects of intellect to be understood are jointly realized (152.7–10).[28] Of course, other fundamental principles of Aristotle's theory are also invoked in the course of Alexander's elaborate dialectic, most importantly the understanding of pleasure as the natural and inevitable accompaniment of the unimpeded actualization of a natural capacity intrinsic to the nature of an animal species.

There is, then, an elaborate network of Aristotelian theory woven all through the essay—hardly a surprise, since Alexander is not only a master apologist for Aristotelianism but also a master scholar of the subject. His authoritative, even imperialistic, use of this theory emerges effortlessly in the essay—there is a seductive air of inevitability whenever a key Aristotelian concept is invoked. But every empire, even intellectual empires, will have subjects whose lives are not just governed but also coopted by the imperial system. And here this role is played by Epicureans and Stoics. After concluding that pleasure makes sense as a neonatal object of attachment but that this is only so because it is an apparent good relative to the merely perceptual nature of animals, Alexander neatly skewers both of his opponents (152.31–35):

> And even if it is consistent for others who say that this is the first object of attachment because their theories must be internally consistent, nevertheless since *they* have not made divisions and distinctions *some* of them say that the primary object of attachment is us, and *others* say that it is the external pleasant object; but none of them put the two aspects together and finished the whole theory. At any rate, both groups taken together make a sound claim while each taken separately makes an unsound claim.

In a way, it took Aristotle to "put the two aspects together and finish the whole theory"—but only Aristotle as interpreted by Alexander against the background of 500 years of intellectual progress, and only an Aristotle with the foresight to synthesize theories that emerged long after his own death!

There isn't time to do much more with this fascinating essay, which illustrates what is most important about Alexander's intellectual methodology. But before closing, I should add just one or two small points. First, Alexander doesn't just outflank his opponents. He also deals explicitly (as the essay's title suggests) with the Aristotelian theorists who have preceded him in his mission to revive, restate, and renew Aristotelian ethics for the then modern world. Early in the essay (151.3) we meet the first of these Aristotelian theories—attributed to Xenarchus and Boethus, intellectual leaders in the school during the vital transitional decades between the Hellenistic and Imperial worlds.[29] Their view isn't sharp enough for Alexander, though they had the good sense (in Alexander's estimation) to base their views on book 8 of the *Nicomachean Ethics*. And then a second group (151.18) comes along, inspired (at least in Alexander's view) by a different move made in the *Nicomachean Ethics*. But the most promising (though still inadequate) theory emerged from the analyses of Verginius Rufus and his predecessor Sosicrates (151.30 ff.); this strategy involved a clever deployment of the teleological naturalism which was later the backbone of Alexander's ultimate solution—and he shows how one of *their* key principles also comes from the works of the master, *Nicomachean Ethics* 10, in fact. Alexander's own solution is even more wide-ranging and makes use not only of the naturalism of the Aristotelian tradition but also of other familiar Aristotelian distinctions, most prominently that between the good and the apparent good. This is put to a wholly new use here, mapped onto the natural motivation to pursue the true good (which only a mature human can grasp) and the developmentally preliminary attachment to the apparent good seen in pre-rational animals. This is how Stoic virtue and Epicurean pleasure are shown each to be partial answers to the problem of the "primary object of attachment"—a problem set for philosophers long after Aristotle's death but which, inevitably it seems, only Aristotelian ethics could solve.

Finally, I return to my claim that Alexander's naturalism is a vital part of the story of Aristotelian ethics, that we can address the challenge of identifying the end and goal of human life in a way that affirms its rational character, the special place for virtue, and the distinctive active-ness of the best human life—all without ever invoking a super-natural, cosmological, or theological principle, drawing only on general principles applicable to the sublunary world as a whole. And this Alexander does. There is, of course, no god in this essay, no allusion to what is divine in us, to how godlike contemplation is, to the gap between sub- and superlunary worlds, to our need to *athanatizein* if we are to be the best possible humans. Epicureans avoided supernaturalism too, but only (on the view standard in non-Epicurean circles) by abandoning the specialness of human excellence. Stoics had to cheat, if only by invoking a divine cosmic nature alongside human nature. And as for the Platonists—well, god was all over their conception of the goal of life. It was only going to get worse (or better, depending on your prior convictions) in the centuries to follow. Alexander was, as I have suggested, even more of a naturalistic thinker than Aristotle himself. Two short texts from the conclusion of Alexander's essay illustrate this.

First, he is explicit in holding that natural principles alone suffice to account for the critical aspects of Aristotelian ethics (153.16–21):

> For it is not as though a man is first pleased and then as a result comes to desire that through which he was pleased. For nature is not in need of its own distinct reasoning [*oikeios logos*] but rather, for natural entities without exception, a starting point of this kind [i.e., natural] is followed by its consequences and by an end of the same kind, providing that there is no impediment, the end not being the result of planning, as in the case of the crafts, but rather just being built that way. The end

as Aristotle states it (that is, activity according to virtue) is in harmony with this kind of starting point.

Note again the explicit use of the alignment thesis which I have suggested is the key to later Peripatetic naturalism—though it derives from Carneadean dialectic and is absent from Aristotle's theory until Alexander goes to work on putting it there. And even more revealing, note how emphatic Alexander is about the naturalness of the teleology. Far from relying lazily on the craft/nature parallel, which has its origins in the Platonic craftsman god and which (in my view) Aristotle himself sometimes leans on too readily, Alexander goes on the offensive with the articulation of a view that Aristotle would of course share, though he would never thematize it so forcefully. The *telos* which is so deeply embedded is not "the result of planning"; that is, it is free of providence or *pronoia*.[30] Unlike a Platonist or any Stoic, Alexander is (like his master, I believe, but more consistently) ready to deny that nonnatural providence in any form is needed to account for the special hold that virtue has on human beings. I suggested earlier that Piso tried and failed to get this result. Alexander, with his mastery of the Aristotelian tradition, eventually succeeded.

At the beginning of this little book I argued—how persuasively is for others to say—that ethics after Aristotle in both senses (ethics worked out in Aristotle's mode and in his wake) had more to offer to us by opening up fresh perspectives on ethical naturalism than by elaborating on the various virtues and excellences with which contemporary virtue ethics, the most prominent kind of contemporary neo-Aristotelianism, engages itself. For better or worse, that has been a major concern (though not the exclusive focus) of these pages and it is this feature of Alexander's neo-Aristotelian theory which stands out here.

One of the most important and persuasive aspects of Aristotle's naturalism in ethics is his ability to include pleasure as a key component of the virtuous life without compromising or sliding into hedonism (as his friend Eudoxus had done). Alexander admired that in Aristotle. So do I and so, I suspect, do most of us who admire Aristotle's rational naturalism. What's more, I admire Alexander for admiring it in Aristotle. So there is no better way to conclude this book than by quoting Alexander quoting Aristotle (*NE* 10.4, 1175a10–17) on just this point:

> One might well think [said Aristotle] that all humans desire pleasure because all of them also strive to be alive. Life is an activity and each person is active in relation to the objects and with the faculties that he likes best. . . . And pleasure completes those activities, as it also completes being alive, which they desire. So it is reasonable that they strive for pleasure. For it completes being alive for each human being, and this is precisely what is worth choosing.

Notes

1. Working in the Wake of Genius

1. In so doing I am acutely aware that I follow in the footsteps of distinguished and truly learned predecessors, not least Robert Sharples, whose career was devoted to the history of later Aristotelianism; Julia Annas, whose path-breaking *Morality of Happiness* (1993) has been a constant inspiration to my work; and of course Fritz Wehrli and Paul Moraux, who did so much to build the historical and textual foundation on which most contemporary work must rest. I should also note here that Szaif 2012, published after the lectures were delivered, came to my attention too late to affect the main argument significantly (though little of what I have to say would be seriously affected by Szaif's discussion); in what follows I have tried to take account of it where it is possible and where it matters most.

2. Sextus Empiricus *Adversus Mathematicos* 7.16.

3. Anscombe 1958.

4. Though the influence of MacIntyre 1981 has also been great.

5. Hursthouse 2012.

6. See Bobonich 2006 and Kenny 1978.

7. For which Annas 1993 is the best general overview.

8. On which see, e.g., Nehamas 2010 and Whiting 2006.

9. I should record here my appreciation for the wonderful work by Nielsen 2012 and Gill 2012 on a closely related topic, the reception of the *Nicomachean Ethics* in

the Hellenistic and early Imperial periods. My interest in these lectures (which were conceived and delivered before their work appeared) is not so much in the reception of the *NE* as it is in the broader question of how Aristotle's followers responded to his program in ethics.

10. In the series Oxford Readings in Philosophy (Crisp and Slote 1997).

11. The significance of this argument for Aristotle's ethical system is subject to debate and disagreement, of course. Annas 1993 p. 144 argues that its role is smaller than I here claim for it.

12. Foot 2001 p. 39. More generally, Foot 2001 chs. 2 and 3 set up the framework that I have most immediately in mind when talking about Aristotle's "naturalism" and that of later Aristotelians.

13. She does not, of course, efface completely the special character of human good, though it is to be understood in the same naturalistic framework as that which governs other living things. She holds that "human good is *sui generis*. Nevertheless, I maintain that a common conceptual structure remains. For there is a 'natural-history story' about how human beings achieve this good as there is about how plants and animals achieve theirs." Foot 2001 p. 51.

14. Thompson 2008.

15. Williams 1985 ch. 3 contains important reflections on the relationship between Aristotle's teleological and naturalistic approach and our focus on ethical norms and practices embedded in our or other societies.

16. Lynch 1972 pp. 76–81 and passim emphasizes the atmosphere of openness that internal criticism and debate fostered in the Lyceum (as also in the Academy); he suggests (p. 78) that Aristotle deliberately chose Theophrastus over Eudemus to succeed him on the grounds that Eudemus was too orthodox and loyal to Aristotelian views. The third head, Strato, was similarly independent-minded. For a general overview of the characteristics and sociopolitical situation of philosophical schools in Hellenistic Athens, see the lucid and comprehensive survey Habicht 1988.

17. Annas 1993 has outlined many of the central lines of development in ancient eudaimonism.

18. See Sedley 1989.

19. As will become clear, one major focus of disagreement with Annas lies in her assumption (1993 p. 413) that hedonistic developments among later

Aristotelians are basically un-Aristotelian. Many, of course, share her view, which finds its first expression in Cicero.

20. At *Lucullus* 132 the claim is made programmatically by Cicero as a character in the dialogue; also *On Goals* 4.14 and 5.15.

21. See recently Szaif 2012 pp. 17–32, whose survey extends beyond what I sketch here.

22. That the *Magna Moralia* (*MM*) is not a genuine work of Aristotle's, not even a set of notes based on lectures from the master taken down by a student, is the clear current consensus, though there are still some who champion the view that the *MM* is to some degree "authentic." It seems to me, on balance, to be more like some of the pseudo-Aristotelian *Problems* or the *De Mundo* than anything else. See most recently Szaif 2012 p. 17.

23. As with most Hellenistic Peripatetics, the main evidence is collected in Wehrli 1967. But for Lycon and Hieronymus we have a recent collection and study by many hands, Fortenbaugh and White 2004.

24. My appreciation for the importance of Critolaus does not extend to postulating a newly established school, the Neoperipatetics (*Jungperipatetiker*) or to recognizing a "revival" of some sort (contra Szaif 2012 p. 19 and others).

25. Preserved in Stobaeus and recently translated in its entirety for the first time by Sharples. It is text 15A in Sharples 2010. Szaif 2012 pp. 20–22 dates the work to the first century BCE, a traditional but unpersuasive dating, and regards the work as little more than a compilation of other materials. The arguments for such an early date are inconclusive at best and in my judgement remain implausible; similarly, the claim that it is a mere compilation will not, I am persuaded, stand up to careful and sympathetic analysis. Szaif retains the attribution of this account and the Stoic account which precedes it in Stobaeus to Arius Didymus; unlike him, pp. 20–21, I think that these assumptions make rather a large difference to how we interpret the Peripatetic philosophical work, and so I have been rather more cautious on the matter.

26. And indeed, if Anthony Kenny is not mistaken, the definitive formation of the *Nicomachean Ethics* as we now know it. See Kenny 1978 pp. 29–36; more gingerly, Barnes 1999 pp. 18–21.

27. His approach was novel, certainly, and at the very least an updating of Aristotle to take account of Stoic compatibilism; but I think that the late Michael Frede

was right to hold, in his Sather Lectures (Frede 2011), that it was an unsuccessful notion of free will, scarcely coherent, in fact.

28. Owen 1971–1972 p. 136. In this brilliant discussion, Owen hopes "to show that they are too divergent to be incompatible." Like many, I am not persuaded. The conflict is one of the most interesting things about the two discussions, and it is easier to concede their incompatibility if one regards the account in the common book as being Eudemian in origin.

29. See also Moss 2012 for another approach to the role of pleasure in Aristotle's ethics which is so prominent as to raise the concern that his view might be properly characterized as hedonistic.

30. Cf. *EE* 2.1.

31. Annas 1993 chs. 3–4.

32. See Russell 2012.

33. See *Nicomachean Ethics* I.9, 1100a4–9.

34. See Inwood and Woolf 2013 pp. xviii–xix.

35. Nevertheless, Stoic disagreement with Aristotle on the passions did become a very important issue in the early Imperial period. Unfortunately, I will have to skim over this issue very briskly when I come to it.

36. Cicero certainly thought that hedonistic inclinations were incompatible with real Aristotelianism, but he spoke as a follower of Plato in saying so; many in the school disagreed.

37. 436.4 in Fortenbaugh et al. 1992. In the discussion of Theophrastus I use the numbering of this collection.

38. 436.1, 2, 3. In 437 we learn from a stray remark in Athenaeus (*Deipnosophists* 15.15, 637e–f) that the early imperial commentator Adrastus wrote something (it is not clear what) at some length (six books) comparing some aspects of the *peri ēthōn* with Aristotle's *NE*.

39. 436.5–14, 23, 24, 26–28, 32.

40. 436.15.

41. 436.16.

42. 436.17.

43. 436.18, 19, 21, 25, 29–30, 31.

44. 436.33.

45. 438–448.

46. 479–485. On this topic Theophrastus differed significantly from Dicaearchus (on whom see McConnell 2012).
47. 487–498.
48. It is also evident in Theophrastus 441–444; pleasure and pain are central to the function of passions in human life, also an Aristotelian view.
49. Pp. 52–53 Ziegler. Translation from Fortenbaugh et al. 1992.
50. Though Aristotle may have flirted with a similar or even more extreme view in his *Protreptic*, a popular work. See fr. 10b Ross. If we think that Aristotle seriously proposed a dualistic view of this kind before he adopted his characteristic hylomorphic view on the relationship between body and soul, then on this issue too we see Theophrastus working out his own position within the framework of Aristotle's complicated and developing views.
51. In fact, if Theophrastus really was responding to Democritus (as pseudo-Plutarch suggests) a *Protreptic* would be a quite plausible place for such a passage to have occurred.
52. It is possible that his views on the passions reflect an awareness of doctrines later marked as Stoic, but also possible that this appearance is a reflection of the interests of our sources, who naturally compared Peripatetic views with Stoic doctrines on this topic. See 448 (= *Light of the Soul* B ch. 63, On wisdom E) on *apatheia* and 447 (= Barlaam 2.13–14), which suggests that Theophrastus classified passions as being either dependent on opinions, and so voluntary, or not dependent on opinions, in which case they would be unrelated to virtue, vice, and happiness.
53. Explicitly at 2.3.17; see chapter 2 below. See also Dillon 1983.
54. If we are to believe our evidence, the following scholium on *NE* 6.13 1145a10–11 (fr. 461); I use the translation from Fortenbaugh et al. 1992.
55. Russell 2010 has an excellent discussion of this problem.
56. Despite the rather pious view taken by John of Lydia in 490 (= *On the Months* 4.7).
57. On this development in the school, see Annas 1993 ch. 19.
58. Mostly a variety of texts from Cicero, including *Lucullus* 134, *Tusculan Disputations* 5.24–25, 85; *On Goals* 5.12, 77, 85–86; *Academica* 1.33, 35; *On the Laws* 1.37–38.
59. This may also be the right way to consider the claim made by Aspasius (fr. 533 = *in Nic. Eth.* 19.1, p. 178 Heilbut), on a topic about which Aristotle's statements

are so complicated that one must be uncertain about his final view. There are three kinds of friendship, based on pleasure, utility, and virtue. And there are friendships based on equality and those based on superiority. But are there such asymmetrical friendships in all three species of *philia?* Theophrastus and Eudemus say yes, but then they face the problem which may have complicated Aristotle's view—are not virtuous people equal *qua* virtuous? If so, and if we are virtue friends, are we not equal? If so, how can we be in an asymmetrical friendship? To give a respectable answer Theophrastus may have to squirm a bit, that is, to equivocate; it turns out that such asymmetry comes about only when there is an antecedent and independent basis for the asymmetry (husband and wife, ruler and ruled, father and son)—if people already in that sort of asymmetrical relationship subsequently become virtuous, there is both an asymmetry and a virtue friendship—but not in the same respect. This looks very much like an awkward attempt to extract a tidier view from Aristotle's theory, at the price of evasive qualifications rather than clear disagreement.

60. Originally entitled *On Principles:* on the nature and title of Theophrastus's *Metaphysics,* see the introduction to Laks and Most 1993, esp. ix–xviii.

61. It is worth comparing the willingness of the author of the *MM* to entertain, though perhaps not to endorse fully, the view that it would be absurd for god to be a self-contemplator; unlike Aristotle, the author dismisses the issue as irrelevant to ethics (2.15.4–5, 1213a4–10). In this passage the author shows clear awareness of the argument of *Metaphysics* 12 that god can only contemplate himself.

2. Flirting with Hedonism

1. See also 1.5–8 esp. 1.8.2 (1186a32–34). On *metriopatheia* see also Dillon 1983 and Bonazzi 2009.

2. See for example 2.4.2, 2.6.39, 2.7.28–31, 2.10.5, 2.11.49; there are few such examples of direct binary pairing of *logos* and *pathos* in the work of Aristotle himself.

3. See *EE* 1215b6, 1216a11, *NE* 1141b3, 1179a13.

4. *MM* 1.1.7; 1.1.26, 1.20.4, 1.34.25, 2.6.2.

5. Cf. 2.7.29–30 = 1206b7–21 and 1.19.3 (where the deletion of 1190b7–8 in some mss. is clearly not warranted).

6. Though it is in fact impossible to prove that Hieronymus wrote later than Magnus rather than at the same time or even earlier.

7. In *Parts of Animals* 1.5.

8. Note also the *hormē pros to philein* at 2.16.3 = 1213b17.

9. This frank acknowledgement clearly anticipates the position later taken by Critolaus on the nature of happiness. See chapter 3.

10. *Tusculan Disputations* 5.24–25, *Academica* 1.33–35, *On Goals* 5.12.

11. "Naturalism" is, of course, a slippery term much used and in a variety of senses. What I refer to here is a commitment to constraining ethical theory by relatively dispassionate observations of actual human life and behavior and a strong tendency to situate one's descriptive account of human nature within a framework that applies equally to other life forms. Aristotle, in my view, qualifies as having strong naturalistic tendencies in this sense. My claim is that his followers take the tendencies further.

12. White 2002. His article is accompanied by my comments (Inwood 2002). Despite my deflationary remarks there, I continue to think that White's discussion is one of the most useful surveys of the themes that I cover in this chapter. His comments on Strato are on p. 74. A more recent discussion of this and later material on happiness can be found in Sharples 2007a.

13. Fr. 134 Wehrli = text 83 in Desclos and Fortenbaugh 2011 = Stobaeus 2.7 p. 54 Wachsmuth.

14. See Inwood 2014.

15. Hence I think that this isolated quotation is more likely to come from Strato's *On Good* than from his *On Happiness.*

16. Though one biography of Aristotle reports that Praxiteles was head between them (Lycon fr. 6 Wehrli = text 3B in Fortenbaugh and White 2004).

17. Lynch 1972 p. 139–140 on Lycon; also Mejer 2004.

18. On his wealth, see Lynch 1972 p. 155, Mejer 2004.

19. Cicero at *TD* 5.13 dismisses him as *rebus ieiunior,* perhaps reflecting little beyond his contempt for Lycon's hedonism.

20. Fr. 10. I think it likely that the puzzling phrase which occurs here (*hōs Leukimos*) is a baffling marginal gloss rather than a corruption of a phrase pertaining to the definition.

21. White 2002 pp. 76–79.

22. It is not even as morally dubious as the view of Heraclides Ponticus (fr. 55 Wehrli), who noted that pleasure was a notable factor in the encouragement and maintenance of certain virtues, such as *megalopsuchia*. It is not difficult to imagine an Aristotelian embracing Heraclides's observations.

23. At *TD* 3.77 Cicero seems to attack Lycon for holding a muddled view, but from the attack we can perhaps learn something. Lycon "played down distress and said that it was provoked by trivial matters, the inconveniences of fortune and the body [i.e, external and bodily *mala*, to put the point in Aristotelian terms] and not by the *mala* of the soul." Cicero cites this view as part of his discussion of Alcibiades's distress at his own lack of virtue—not an issue Lycon was concerned with as far as we know. His denial that we feel distress at our own weaknesses of character suggests that pleasure felt at *ta kala* could well have been pleasure at good character and its activities, as suggested in the text. Presumably he denied that we feel distress at *animi mala* because a person so afflicted would very likely enjoy his own corrupt state or be unaware of it. There is no reason to suggest that he had adopted the Stoic view that only a virtuous agent would be inclined to regret moral failings and such a person has none.

24. Though the term for pleasure, *chara*, may have been borrowed from Stoicism. This is a point on which White puts great emphasis, but it is also possible that this term was adopted independently. It is, after all, not such a rare word that the choice of it can only be explained by Stoic influence.

25. See Sextus *M* 7.227–2312 on the interpretation of *phantasia*.

26. White's discussion (2002 pp. 80–84) includes his comparison of Lycon with Hieronymus. Frr. 4 (= Diogenes Laërtius 4.40-42) and 6 (= Diogenes Laërtius 5.67-68) (in Fortenbaugh and White 2004, cf. Lynch p. 151) establish that Lycon and Hieronymus were rough contemporaries and that there was enmity between them. Hieronymus also criticized Arcesilaus. See also Dalfino 1993. Dalfino gives a useful general survey of Hieronymus's philosophy, emphasizing the degree to which his Peripatetic views have been affected by distinctively Hellenistic influences.

27. Fr. 5 = Diogenes Laërtius 4.42; White 2004 p. 80.

28. Note the likely presence of the Stoic term *katōrthōsai* in the papyrus fragment.

29. Clement of Alexandria, who had some excellent doxographical sources for earlier ethical theory. His information is confirmed by Plutarch who paraphrases his

goal as 'living in *hēsuchia*' (fr. 23 = *St. Rep.* 1033bc); Iamblichus (fr. 15 = *De Anima* in Stobaeus 1.42, pp. 382-3 Wachsmuth) confirms the term *aochlēsia*.

30. For the much stronger move in this direction by Critolaus, see chapter 3.

31. See White 2004 p. 117.

32. White (2004 pp. 120–123) suggests that fr. 13B = *Acad.* 2.138 indicates that Chrysippus may already have taken Hieronymus's formulation of the *telos* as an evasive equivalent for frank hedonism. But this text may have an Antiochean origin, so its fidelity to Chrysippus can be questioned. And there is no reason to think that Hieronymus was the only philosopher to have taken an undisturbed life as the goal.

33. This formulation is also found at fr. 18B = *On Goals* 2.16.

34. It is bizarre to claim that Epicurus separated virtue from the goal altogether, when he held that the goal is pleasure and that it is impossible to live pleasantly without living virtuously—and vice versa (Principle Doctrine 5, one of the best known maxims of the school). So we had best bracket out Cicero's antihedonistic slurs and focus on more credible, though still speculative, lines of reasoning.

35. White 2002 p. 81; my discussion is at Inwood 2002 pp. 96–99.

36. White 2002 p. 82.

37. As White recognizes but passes over (2002 p. 82).

38. Diogenes Laërtius 7.37.

39. White 2002 p. 83.

40. The debate between these two Peripatetics was of great interest to Cicero, who is the source for most of our information on the issue. See McConnell 2012. For the texts, see Wehrli 1967, Heft I, fragments 25–46. Dicaearchus is presented in the tradition as being dedicated to the practical life whereas Theophrastus (and Aristotle, though he is less often mentioned) preferred the theoretical life. Cicero's emphasis on Theophrastus's preference for the purely theoretical life is to some extent a product of the sharp contrast with Dicaearchus.

41. Matelli 2004 p. 301 argues that Hieronymus's time in Athens was early in his life, while Strato was head of the school, and overlapped with the life of Epicurus; she suggests that his ethical work fits well in this period of his life and that when he returned to Rhodes he turned his attention to other themes (2004 pp. 307–310). Her account of the political maneuverings of dynasties and

schools in the Aegean basin during his lifetime provides a plausible context for a philosopher to prefer a politically quiet and withdrawn life.

42. Plutarch *St. Rep.* 1033bc (= Hieronymus fr. 23 and text 23, p. 143 in White 2004) cites Epicurus and Hieronymus as quietists when he chides Chrysippus and other Stoics for not living according to their own ideal of the practical life.

43. I focus on the Epicureans here, for they were certainly the foremost exponents of hedonism in the period. But as Tony Long reminds me, Cyrenaic hedonism also played a role in the developing debates of the Hellenistic period; their distinctive approach to hedonism is reflected in book 10 of Diogenes Laërtius, where it is contrasted to that of Epicurus. Cyrenaics are also brought into the framework of the *Carneadea divisio.* A general concern with hedonism should not surprise us. Not only is it an important feature of Aristotle's own ethical thought, but Plato himself, whose dialogues represent several different approaches to pleasure, emphasizes in his late and influential *Philebus* the importance of pleasure in the best human life.

44. This is the focus of Prodicus's Choice of Heracles, *Memorabilia* 2.1; it is this book which is alleged to have brought Zeno to philosophy (D.L. 7.2).

45. Gigante 1999.

46. I say this of Seneca despite his openness to certain Epicurean themes in the early books of his collection of letters. For the most part, Seneca's hostility to Epicureanism is of a piece with what we find in the rest of the later ancient tradition. Seneca was also interested in Epicurus as a literary predecessor (see Inwood 2007b).

47. Cicero is our main, but not our only, source for these events. See Powell 1995 pp. 13–14.

3. The Turning Point

1. Striker 1986.

2. Burnyeat 1997.

3. Stobaeus *Ecl.* 2.7 p. 76 Wachsmuth; Clement *Stromates* 2.21; Plutarch *Comm. Not.* ch. 27.

4. SVF 3.12 = Galen *PHP* 5.6; Stobaeus Ecl. 2.7 p. 76 Wachsmuth. SVF 3.13–15 = Cicero *Fin.* 4.14, 2.34, 3.31). See Inwood 2007.

5. On Diodorus of Tyre see Hahm 2007 p. 68, *On Goals* 5.14.
6. See Hahm 2007 pp. 51–52, 89–91, Sharples 2002 pp. 14, 22–24, Sharples 2007 p. 508 n. 13, and also Sharples 2007a esp. pp. 628–629.
7. See Hahm 2007 pp. 95–96.
8. Philo, *Aet. Mundi.* 6.90, 94 = frr. 12–13 Wehrli.
9. Stobaeus *Ecl.* I.103 W. = fr. 14 Wehrli.
10. Stobaeus *Ecl.* I.1 p. 35 Wachsmuth, Tertullian *De Anima* 5.1 and Macrobius *In Somn.* I.14.20 = frr. 16–18 Wehrli.
11. This is a view which Antiochus seems to have taken up from Critolaus and attributed to the early Academy as a whole. See Cicero *Acad.* I.26, I.39.
12. Hahm 2007 pp. 55–56. Two main reasons seem to have been given for denying it the status of a craft: rhetoric is not in fact necessary for success in public speaking; and rhetoric is not socially beneficial. These normative considerations stand in contrast to Aristotle's approach to determining what counts as a *technē.*
13. Inwood 2014.
14. SVF 3.56 (Antipater) = Clement *Stromates* 5.14.
15. Hahm 2007, White 2002, Sharples 2010 pp. 166–8. Evidence of the influence of Critolaus on the Stoics comes at *On Goals* 3.32, where the language of "filling out" is used; this is Critolaus's terminology (see below).
16. Accepting the emendation of *progonikên* to *trigenikên.*
17. Doubtless the term and the idea behind it were partly inspired by Aristotle's use of *sunarithmeisthai* (*NE* 1097b17) but the difference is significant. It is used in an important passage of Plutarch (*De communibus notitiis* 1069f) which seems to owe something to the earlier use by Critolaus. The word is not a new coinage; only the sense is novel.
18. Fr. 19 = Stobaeus *Ecl.* 2.7, p. 46 Wachsmuth.
19. Although, as Tim Clarke has reminded me, the goods of the soul he has in mind could have included activities as well as dispositions and capacities. Nevertheless, the absence of any direct mention of activities, let alone his apparent failure to make activities *central* to his notion of the *telos,* is a striking difference from what we see in Aristotle. Szaif 2012, part II, is rightly sensitive to the importance of the difference between an emphasis on "filling out" a life with goods and an emphasis on activities. However, Szaif has a tendency to conflate the so-called *sumplērōma* thesis with Aristotle's rather different talk of "parts" of happiness

(2012, p. 155–158, esp. n. 14; also p. 176), a tendency which inevitably blunts our appreciation for the originality of Hellenistic developments. Szaif 2012, pp. 157–160, helpfully includes a discussion of the rejection of Critolaus's approach by the commentator Aspasius.

20. Stobaeus *Ecl.* 2.7 p. 46 Wachsmuth = text 18 I in Sharples 2010.
21. The reference here to employment (*to chrēstikon*) of goods also reflects the use of *chrēsis* in the *Magna Moralia*. See Hahm 2007, pp. 68–71.
22. Translation by Sharples 2010, 15 A, with changes = *Ecl.* 2.7.14 pp. 126–7 Wachsmuth. Cf. Szaif 2012 pp. 173–176.
23. See *Eudemian Ethics* 1214a30–33.
24. Gellius *NA* 9.5.6 = fr. 23 Wehrli.
25. White 1992.
26. On Antiochus in this connection, see Bonazzi 2009.
27. I would like to take this occasion to thank Charles Brittain for some exceptionally helpful discussions of book 5 of *On Goals*, and of Cicero generally.
28. Barnes 1997 is the most significant of these.
29. The connection to happiness is even more explicit at *On Goals* 5.83.
30. See Inwood 1995, pp. 660–661. A similar motivation may underlie the distinctive presentation of Stoic ethics in Arius Didymus (op. cit. pp. 654–655); doxography, like debate, calls for homgenization of conceptual frameworks.
31. Annas 2007 and Algra 1997.
32. See Brunschwig 1986.
33. See Striker 1996 ch. 12, section 5, especially p. 269.
34. Lennox 1994 discusses the rather puzzling fact that we have so little evidence that Aristotle's biology was well known in the Hellenistic era; see below on the significance of Piso's speech in *On Goals* 5.
35. Brunner 2010.
36. The Peripatetic nature of this account has been explored in Tsouni 2010, a dissertation whose wider dissemination I look forward to in the near future. I am not persuaded of the essentially Theophrastan character of the book 5 account as Tsouni is, but the argument for its broadly Aristotelian nature is very strong.
37. This nesting of Peripatetic doctrines in the framework of a natural-development theory (of *oikeiôsis*) derived from Stoicism is also a feature of the (probably early Imperial) doxography C preserved in Stobaeus, which also includes a critical

reaction to Critolaus's omission of activity from his Aristotelianism. I will discuss this in the next chapter.

38. Inwood 1984 p. 175.

39. See Tsouni 2010, who thinks that the ultimate origin of the material in the Antiochean account is Theophrastan.

40. The fact that Piso's largely Antiochean account (derived ultimately from Critolaus, as I have argued) is characterized as having characteristics inconsistent with Theophrastus's theory is one of the main reasons for skepticism about an attempt to credit it with an essentially or exclusively Theophrastan inspiration.

41. Cf. Barnes 1989 p. 65, who points to *On Goals* 5.8 and suggests that Piso explicitly claims Staseas as a source at *On Goals* 5.75. I think this slightly misrepresents what Piso says at 5.75, but Barnes draws the right conclusion from 5.8 (though he seems not to notice that it is the character Cicero who invokes Staseas with sympathy in *both* passages). Szaif 2012 pp. 24–25 (esp. n. 21) dismisses Barnes's observation and the possibility of any role at all for Staseas's views with a puzzling dogmatism; he seems unaware of what I take to be the complexities of the position presented by Piso on book 5 and insensitive to the significance of the changes of character.

42. See Moraux 1973 volume I, pp. 217–221. At p. 218 Moraux seems to think that Piso's more rigorist position on happiness means that Staseas cannot be the origin for any part of his account. This, like my own suggestion, is pure speculation.

4. Bridging the Gap

1. For example, Frede 1999 pp. 771–2. The same division is accepted by Sharples and Sorabji 2007; volume 2 of this work has a section of ten chapters (pp. 501–637) on Peripatetics in this period.

2. See Long 2002 p. 218.

3. For a bit of historical context relevant to the practice of philosophy at Athens in the post-Hellenistic period, see Oliver 1977 and 1983. It is often said that the schools ceased to exist at Athens in this period, until the time of the foundation of philosophical chairs in the second century CE, but this is evidently not exactly true nor is it the whole story. That said, Athens certainly ceased to be the

primary locus of serious philosophical activity after the mid first century BCE at the latest and for some time after that.

4. Kenny 1978 pp. 29–36; on Aspasius, see also Alberti and Sharples 1999, Sorabji 2007.

5. Falcon 2012 pp. 11–25 and Falcon 2013, especially pp. 88–91 on ethics. On the question of when and why the Peripatetic commentary movement got under way, I am more sympathetic to the views of Falcon and of Barnes 1997 than to Szaif 2012 pp. 26–27, who retains an older view that has been subject to critical reassessment in recent years.

6. At around the same time another Aristotelian was active, Nicolaus of Damascus. Though he is important for the development of later Aristotelian natural science (as is Xenarchus), we know virtually nothing of his contribution to ethics. See Gottschalk 1987 pp. 1122–1125, Sharples 2007 pp. 509–510.

7. *On Passions* and the *Virtues and Vices* both display another feature of early Imperial ethics also prominent in Doxography C, growing reliance on divisions and categorizations (rather than argument) to articulate doctrine. See Inwood 2014 and Sharples 2007 p. 510. On the emotions in this period Sorabji 2007 is not particularly helpful, since he focusses exclusively on Aspasius.

8. See Karamanolis 2006. Plutarch's little treatise blends Platonic and Aristotelian theory in a number of ways that anticipate the "middle" Platonic approach of, for example, Alcinous; the most striking is his use of Aristotle's form/matter distinction to explicate and give metaphysical detail to the *logos/pathos* polarity. It was significant and controversial within the school to adopt Aristotelian ethical theory in this way; Atticus, for example, violently rejected the entire Aristotelian approach as inconsistent with the spirit of Platonism.

9. See Göransson 1995 and Inwood 1996 for discussion. See more recently Falcon 2012 pp. 11–12 and n. 2. Reference is made there to earlier discussions in the literature. An exceptionally important contribution is Annas 1990. Trapp 2007, while often very informative on developments in later Peripatetic ethics, has little to say on Doxography C or on later Peripatetic theories of *oikeiōsis*. See also Sharples 2007 pp. 508–509 and 2007a pp. 629–634. Szaif 2012 pp. 20–22 retains an older view of the date and characteristics of this material.

10. *Pace* Göransson, the content of the doxography more or less guarantees an approximately Augustan date for it, even if Arius is not the author's name.

11. In this way, too, Alexander will be a fitting conclusion to the tradition; his corpus is littered with probably anonymous works written in his school and under his influence, but unlikely to be directly and exclusively from his own pen.

12. This characterization of the work and its author (and its date) has recently been challenged by Szaif 2012 (see esp. pp. 229–263), a book which unfortunately appeared too late for me to take full account of its argument. My own approach to the topic is, at all events, quite different from his.

13. In chapter 5 we will return briefly to Xenarchus as a figure who made an interesting contribution to the debate about the naturalistic foundations of ethics.

14. *NE* 2.1, 1103a17, *EE* 2.2, 1220b1.

15. See Görgemanns 1983 pp. 166–168.

16. This integration with the *Politics* is a feature of the *Nicomachean* rather than the *Eudemian Ethics*. It is, however, worth considering the possibility that the material on politics and household management which begins at section 26 (p. 147 line 26 Wachsmuth) constitutes a separate doxographical report. As Tad Brennan and Charles Brittain have suggested in discussion, the wording of the transitional paragraph (pp. 147.26–148.4) is very similar to the passage which marks the end of Doxography B (p. 116.15–18). Certainty is not possible.

17. On this aspect of Doxography C, see also Inwood forthcoming, from parts of which some of what follows has been adapted.

18. See Sedley 2007 pp. 194–203.

19. Again, see the discussion in section 5 of "Following Nature" in Striker 1996.

20. For what follows, see also Sharples 2007a pp. 633–634, which includes references to much of the earlier literature on this passage. Particularly with regard to its possible "sources" there has been a very large but ultimately inconclusive discussion in the scholarly literature.

21. Aristotle *NE* 9.9, *EE* 7.12.5 ff.

22. The fundamental point about our natural attachment to our body and soul (the two "parts" of ourself) does structure the exposition of things that are *per se* choiceworthy through to the end of chapter 13 at *Ecl.* 2.124.13. Harry here endeavors to connect such values to the basic orientation to our body and soul set out in this initial passage.

23. Since Aristotle holds in the *De Anima* that soul is a set of capacities in a suitable body and that it is therefore a form (*eidos*) and that form is prior to matter, it

would follow that since we are the hylomorphic compound of soul and body we are most essentially this set of capacities. When Aristotle says that we are our *nous* most of all (*NE* 9.8, 1168b29–1169a3) he does not mean our immaterial *nous* (if we have one), which is not the actualization of a capacity.

24. For this point I am particularly grateful to the Berkeley workshop in ancient philosophy (April 2013) for their critical response to my original and less plausible version of the point.

25. Usually translated as "principles," but I prefer a more deflationary and etymological translation. It is worth stressing that these starting points do not seem to be intended to provide an account of what virtue ultimately is or of the intrinsic value it comes to have in the life of a developed moral agent (later in his account the virtues are recognized as being intrinsically valuable). But the instrumental starting point for this development represents an approach to Aristotelian ethics with which Aristotle himself would surely have been uncomfortable.

26. For Seneca's relationship to them, see Inwood 2005 chapter I.

27. And this is true even of the otherwise ground-breaking discussion by Christopher Gill (Gill 2012).

28. Glibert-Thirry 1977.

29. See Inwood 2014. For the role of Platonists in the debate about the passions, see Dillon 1983.

30. Despite the fact that Crantor is the earliest known philosopher to use this argument, it came to be thought of as characteristically Aristotelian. Even Philodemus regarded it as Aristotelian; see Gigante 1999 pp. 83–4.

31. For simplicity we can slide over their metaphysical and methodological significance in book I of the *De Anima*, where he gives his dialectical definition of anger as a desire for causing retaliatory pain (403a30).

32. On the *TD* and several other aspects of the present discussion, see also Nussbaum 1994, especially chapters 9–11.

33. Though there is nothing distinctively Stoic about defining anger as a kind of desire for revenge; see *De Anima* 403a30–31, where Aristotle gives as an example of the dialectician's mode of answering the *ti esti* question: "a desire for inflecting pain in return, or something of the sort." This is clearly not a proper definition nor does Aristotle say that it is; it is cited by Aristotle as a

typical answer of the sort that a dialetician might give. Stoic and other parallels are given by Glibert-Thirry 1977 (volume 2 p. 290) à propos of pseudo-Andronicus IV.

34. For this text, see Glibert-Thirry 1977 p. 231 . Glibert-Thirry (1977 p. 34 and Part I ch. III) suggests that the compiler of this work may have been a professional rhetor rather than a philosopher, but the only support offered for this proposal is the work's apparent lack of philosophical integrity, i.e., its blending of definitions from different schools and its organization into lists of definitions and divisions. Rather than marking it as a rhetorical work, though, this seems to place it firmly within a tradition of philosophical handbook writing.

35. Glibert-Thirry (1977) pp. 290–292.

36. Here I offer a different account of how the debate developed in the Hellenistic period than does Gill (2012).

37. A parallel case in illustration is worth citing. In the *Timaeus* 75cd, Plato's craftsman god had no choice but to make our skulls thin and fragile—it was a necessary tradeoff to achieve the good outcome of higher intelligence.

38. Plutarch *On Stoic Self-Contradictions* 1044d.

39. Credited to Posidonius, I.2.3, if we may accept the supplement based on Lactantius's imitation.

40. I use John Procopé's vivid translation for the *De Ira* (in Cooper and Procopé 1995) as I use Margaret Graver's for the *Tusculans* (Graver 2002).

41. I am unaware of any pertinent parallel in Latin for the significance of biting one's own lips (Pliny the Elder 11.84 is not to the point, though it will come up in word searches: it describes spiders biting other animals' lips) and so we have to interpret it in its context to get a sense of its meaning. But perhaps the significance of lip-biting is still open to debate.

42. This is a point that Seneca even comes back to in his letters, which are more often anti-Peripatetic than has been thought—though no one can miss the attack on Peripatetic *metriopatheia* in letters 85 and 116.

43. Inwood 2005.

44. See Inwood 2014.

45. I have analyzed the debates Seneca which constructs in these letters in Inwood 2007a.

5. Alexander and Imperial Aristotelianism

1. This is a view of human nature that Harry could be found embracing in his treatise, as we noted in the previous chapter.

2. I retain the neuter adjectives *aülon* and *akraton* of the mss; Helmbold accepts Pohlenz's emendation to *aülos* and *akratos.*

3. See Dillon 1993.

4. For an overview of Alexander's achievements and a description of the works in his corpus, see Sharples 1987.

5. See Bobzien 1998 ch. 4.

6. Todd 1976.

7. Bergeron and Dufour 2008; Caston 2012.

8. Sharples 2004, 2008; Dufour 2013.

9. Sharples 1992, 1994, 1990a.

10. Diogenes Laërtius 7.106.

11. Or at least the positive option where the potential is bivalent. See below.

12. The Stoics had accepted the basic validity of this relationship—and here again I can do no better than to refer to Gisela Striker's classic article on this topic (Striker 1986), augmented, perhaps, by one of Seneca's more engrossing letters (number 85), on which I have offered some comment myself in Inwood 2007a.

13. 1168a5–8; 1244b23–29; see also *NE* 10, 1175a11–13.

14. See also Doxography C at *Ecl.* 2.7.13 (118.11–17). Puzzlingly, Szaif 2012 p. 27 regards this as a "doxography" of earlier Peripatetic material rather than as a philosophical essay in its own right. I think a careful analysis justifies the more charitable assessment.

15. Sharples has recently reedited the text of the *Mantissa* in Sharples 2008. His own translation of the text is in Sharples 2004, pp. 150–159. See also Dufour 2013.

16. Alexander indicates the passages conventionally, by quoting the first and last phrases; numerically precise page references are an artifact of modern editions.

17. Contra Bruns 1887 ad loc. (who points to *NE* 2.3, 1104b30), the reference here is probably to *NE* 8.2, 1155b18–19, where Aristotle says that the object of love is either good, pleasant or useful. The wording does not match exactly in either case, but Alexander's general strategy in this essay involves drawing on *NE* 8–10.

18. It is not clear how Alexander thinks the distinction between qualified and unqualified pleasure works against the view he criticizes here.

19. Sosicrates *may* be the Hellenistic historian (and succession-writer) from Rhodes, probably a Peripatetic fellow traveller; he is often cited as a source in Diogenes Laërtius, though it is a surprise that he should be mentioned for his own doctrines here; another possibility is a student of Carneades. As for Verginius Rufus, there are fewer plausible options. The first century CE Roman general known from Tacitus seems a very unlikely identification, but no one has made a better suggestion. See Sharples 2010a p. 146.

20. I retain the ms. reading *noēton*, contra Sharples 2004, 2008 ad loc., who prints the emendation *noēt<ik>on*. My translation leaves open what the object of thought might be, oneself or an external object, but requires that it be in actuality. Sharples translates "being active in respect of intellect and being intelligent in actuality." The emendation, then, makes the two components of the *telos* essentially the same, which renders the text repetitive without clearly improving the sense.

21. Omitting *kai tēn* as a mistaken doublet for *kai zēn* right before it.

22. Alexander is shifting back and forth between the neuter, indicating animals as such, and the masculine, indicating human beings. Clearly the same analysis is meant to apply both to humans and to other animals.

23. 1175a10–17.

24. Alexander here omits the examples which Aristotle uses to illustrate: culture lovers are active in relation to songs with their faculty of hearing, lovers of learning are similarly active with their intellect in relation to *theōrēmata*, etc.

25. See *Fin.* 5.17.

26. See Striker 1996, section 5 of "Following Nature," esp. p. 269. Sharples 2004 notes the significance of what I call the "alignment condition" at pp. 149–150, citing Striker.

27. Aristotle frequently claims that the final cause has two senses, so this too is a general principle of his philosophy, not some special move made in ethics. See *Physics* 194a36–37 and Ross ad loc., *Metaphysics* 1072b1–4, *De Anima* 415b2–3.

28. Alexander may be thinking of the intellect itself as the ultimate object of intellection, which would be a striking piece of Alexander's own metaphysical epistemology, whose relationship to its source in Aristotle's *De Anima* and *Metaphysics* remains controversial. (*De Anima* 3.5 and *Metaphysics* 12.7 are relevant texts.) In

this passage, though, Alexander need be thinking of nothing more than that the intelligible form which is the object of thought is taken into the mind from its source in order to be made an actual object of intellection. But whichever interpretation is right, the key point for my purposes is that Alexander accepts the uniform application of this natural principle to the problem of the *prōton oikeion.*

29. See Falcon 2012 and Falcon 2013 both generally on the transition from the Hellenistic Peripatos to the Imperial age—an account which I find quite persuasive over all—and in particular on this essay by Alexander, including the contributions of Xenarchus, Boethus, Sosicrates, and Verginius Rufus (pp. 42–47, 139–157). Falcon provides a fuller discussion of Alexander's essay than Sharples 2010 is able to present.

30. See Sharples 2002 on the doctrine NSP, "No Sublunary Providence."

Note on the Ancient Texts

Aside from the principal ethical works of Aristotle himself, many of the ancient Aristotelian texts discussed in this book will be relatively obscure to the general reader. For Aristotle (and pseudo-Aristotle, especially the *Magna Moralia*) and other more common ancient authors such as Cicero, Seneca, and Plutarch, readers should have little trouble finding appropriate texts and translations. (Otherwise unattributed translations are my own.) Wehrli 1967 was for a long time the standard collection of fragments and it is still needed for some philosophers (such as Eudemus and Critolaus), but more up-to-date collections are now available for many. I indicate most important of these here in roughly historical sequence; details are given in the bibliography that follows.

Theophrastus of Eresos: Fortenbaugh et al. 1992.

Strato of Lampsacus: Desclos and Fortenbaugh 2011.

Lyco of Troas and Hieronymus of Rhodes: Fortenbaugh and White 2004.

Important fragments of Critolaus (Greek text in Wehrli) and all of "Doxography C" (Greek text in volume 2 of *Stobaeus: Anthologium* eds. Wachsmuth and Hense) can be found in Sharples 2010.

Alexander of Aphrodisias: Sharples 1990a, 1992, 1994, 2004, 2008 and Todd 1976. (The Greek texts can be found in *Commentaria in Aristotelem Graeca* Supp. 2.1–2, ed. Bruns.)

The abbreviation SVF stands for Stoicorum Veterum Fragmenta, ed. H. von Arnim, published by Teubner in Stuttgart (1903–1924).

Bibliography

Alberti, A., and R. Sharples, eds. 1999. *Aspasius: The Earliest Extant Commentary on Aristotle's Ethics.* Berlin: De Gruyter.

Algra, K. 1997. "Chrysippus, Carneades, Cicero: The Ethical *Divisiones* in Cicero's *Lucullus.*" Pp. 107–139 in Inwood and Mansfeld 1997.

Algra, K., J. Barnes, J. Mansfeld, and M. Schofield, eds. 1999. *The Cambridge History of Hellenistic Philosophy.* Cambridge: Cambridge University Press.

Annas, J. 1990. "The Hellenistic Version of Aristotle's Ethics." *Monist* 73, 80–96.

Annas, J. 1993. *The Morality of Happiness.* Oxford: Oxford University Press.

Annas, J. 2007. "Carneades' Classification of Ethical Theories." Pp. 187–223 in Ioppolo and Sedley 2007.

Anscombe G. E. M. 1958. "Modern Moral Philosophy." *Philosophy* 33, 1–19.

Arnim, H. von. 1903-1924. *Stoicorum Veterum Fragmenta.* Teubner: Stuttgart.

Barnes, J. 1989. "Antiochus of Ascalon," ch. 3 of Barnes and Griffin 1989.

Barnes, J. 1997. "Roman Aristotle," ch. 1 of Barnes and Griffin 1997.

Barnes, J., and M. Griffin, eds. 1989. *Philosophia Togata.* Oxford: Oxford University Press.

Barnes, J., and M. Griffin, eds. 1997. *Philosophia Togata II.* Oxford: Oxford University Press.

Barnes, J. 1999. "An Introduction to Aspasius," ch. 1 of *Aspasius: The Earliest Extant Commentary on Aristotle's Ethics.* New York: De Gruyter.

Bergeron, M., and R. Dufour. 2008. *Alexandre d'Aphrodise: De l'âme.* Paris: Vrin.

Bobonich, C. 2006. "Aristotle's Ethical Treatises," ch. I in Kraut 2006.

Bobzien, S. 1998. *Determinism and Freedom in Stoic Philosophy.* Oxford: Oxford University Press.

Bonazzi, M. 2009. "Antiochus' Ethics and the Subordination of Stoicism," pp. 33–54 in *The Origins of the Platonic System: Platonisms of the Early Empire and their Philosophical Contexts,* eds. M. Bonazzi and J. Opsomer (= *Collection d'Études Classiques* 23). Louvain: Peeters.

Boys-Stones, G. R. 2001. *Post-Hellenistic Philosophy: A Study of Its Development from the Stoics to Origin.* Oxford: Oxford University Press.

Brunner, A. 2010. *Totas paginas commovere: Cicero's presentation of Stoic Ethics in De Finibus book 3.* Dissertation, Central European University (Budapest).

Bruns I. ed. 1887. *Commentaria in Aristotelem Graeca* Supp. 2.1–2. Berlin: Reimer.

Brunschwig, J. 1986. "The Cradle Argument in Epicureanism and Stoicism." Pp. 113–144 in Schofield and Striker 1986.

Burnyeat, M. 1997. "Antipater and Self-Refutation: Elusive Arguments in Cicero's *Academica.*" Pp. 277–310 in Inwood and Mansfeld 1997.

Caston, V. 2012. *Alexander of Aphrodisias On the Soul* Part I. London: Bristol Classical Press.

Cooper, J., and J. Procopé, ed. and tr. 1995. *Seneca: Moral and Political Essays.* Cambridge: Cambridge University Press.

Crisp, R., and M. Slote, eds. 1997. *Virtue Ethics.* Oxford: Oxford University Press.

Dalfino, M. C. 1993. "Ieronimo di Rodi: la dottrina della vacuitas doloris." *Elenchus* 14, 277–303.

Desclos, M.-L., and W. W. Fortenbaugh. 2011. *Strato of Lampsacus: Text, Translation, and Discussion* (Rutgers University Studies in Classical Humanities vol. 16). New Brunswick, NJ: Transaction Publishers.

Dillon, J. M. 1996. *The Middle Platonists 80 BC to AD 220.* London: Duckworth. First edition 1977.

Dillon, J. M. 1983. "*Metriopatheia* and *Apatheia:* Some Reflections on a Controversy in Later Greek Ethics." Pp. 508–517 in *Essays in Ancient Greek Philosophy* vol. 2, eds. J. P. Anton and A. Preus. Albany: State University of New York Press.

Dillon, J. M. 1993. *Alcinous: The Handbook of Platonism.* Oxford: Oxford University Press.

Dillon, J. M., and A. A. Long, eds. 1988. *The Question of Eclecticism: Studies in Later Greek Philosophy.* Berkeley: University of California Press.

Donini, P. L. 1982. *Le scuole, l'anima, l'impero: la filosofia antica da Antioco a Plotino.* Torino: Rosenberg and Sellier.

Dufour, R. 2013. *Alexandre d'Aphrodise: de l'âme II (Mantissa).* Québec: Presses de l'Université Laval.

Eliasson, E. 2009. "*Magna Moralia* 1187a29–1187b20: The Early Reception of Aristotle's Notion of Voluntary Action." *Oxford Studies in Ancient Philosophy* 37, 213–244.

Eliasson, E. 2013. "The Account of the Voluntariness of Virtue in the Anonymous Peripatetic Commentary on *Nicomachean Ethics* II–V." *Oxford Studies in Ancient Philosophy* 44, 195–231.

Falcon, A. 2012. *Aristotelianism in the First Century BCE: Xenarchus of Seleucia.* Cambridge: Cambridge University Press.

Falcon, A. 2013. "Aristotelianism in the First Century BC: Xenarchus of Seleucia." Pp. 78–94 in Schofield 2013.

Foot, P. 2001. *Natural Goodness.* Oxford: Oxford University Press.

Fortenbaugh, W. W., ed. 1983. *On Stoic and Peripatetic Ethics: The Work of Arius Didymus* (Rutgers University Studies in Classical Humanities vol. 1). New Brunswick, NJ: Transaction Publishers.

Fortenbaugh, W. W. 1983a. "Arius, Theophrastus, and the *Eudemian Ethics*." Pp. 203–223 in Fortenbaugh 1983.

Fortenbaugh, W. W., et al. 1992. *Theophrastus of Eresus: Sources for His Life, Writings, Thought, and Influence.* Leiden: Brill.

Fortenbaugh, W. W., and S. White, eds. 2004. *Lyco of Troas and Hieronymus of Rhodes* (Rutgers University Studies in Classical Humanities vol. 12). New Brunswick, NJ: Transaction Publishers.

Fortenbaugh, W. W., and Peter Steinmetz, eds. 1989. *Cicero's Knowledge of the Peripatos.* New Brunswick, NJ: Transaction Publishers.

Frede, D., and A. Laks, eds. 2002. *Traditions of Theology.* Boston: Brill.

Frede, M. 1999. "Epilogue." Pp. 771–797 in Algra et al. 1999.

Frede, M. 2011. *A Free Will.* Berkeley: University of California Press.

Furley, D. J. "Comments on Dr. Sharples' Paper: A Note on Arius and *Magna Moralia* 1.1–2." Pp. 160–164 in Fortenbaugh 1983.

Gigante, Marcello. 1999. *Kepos e Peripatos: contributo alla storia dell'aristotelismo antico.* Naples: Bibliopolis.

Gill, C. 2012. "The Transformation of Aristotle's *Ethics* in Roman Philosophy." Pp. 31–52 in Miller 2012.

Glibert-Thirry, A. 1977. *Pseudo-Andronicus de Rhodes "Peri pathōn."* Leiden: Brill.

Göransson, T. 1995. *Albinus, Alcinous, Arius Didymus.* Göteborg: Acta Universitatis Gothoburgensis.

Görgemanns, H. 1983. "*Oikeiōsis* in Arius Didymus." Pp. 165–189 in Fortenbaugh 1983.

Gottschalk, H. B. 1987. "Aristotelian Philosophy in the Roman World from the Time of Cicero to the End of the Second Century AD." Pp. 1079–1174 in *Aufstieg und Niedergang der Römischen Welt* (ed. H. Temporini and W. Haase; De Gruyter: Berlin and New York) ii.36.2.

Gottschalk, H. B. 1990. "The Earliest Aristotelian Commentators," ch. 3 of Sorabji 1990.

Graver, M. tr. and comm. 2002. *Cicero on the Emotions. Tusculan Disputations 3 and 4.* Chicago: University of Chicago Press.

Habicht, C. 1988. *Hellenistic Athens and Her Philosophers* (The 1988 David Magie Lecture at Princeton University). Princeton, NJ: Princeton University Press.

Hahm, D. 2007. "Critolaus and Late Hellenistic Peripatetic Philosophy." Pp. 47–101 in Ioppolo and Sedley 2007.

Hatzimichali, M. 2011. *Potamo of Alexandria and the Emergence of Eclecticism in Late Hellenistic Philosophy.* Cambridge: Cambridge University Press.

Hursthouse, R. 2012. "Virtue Ethics." *The Stanford Encyclopedia of Philosophy* (Summer 2012), ed. Edward N. Zalta. http://plato.stanford.edu/archives/sum2012/entries/ethics-virtue/.

Inwood, B. 1983. "Comments on Professor Görgemanns' Paper." Pp. 190–201 in Fortenbaugh 1983.

Inwood, B. 1984. "Hierocles: Theory and Argument in the Second Century AD." *Oxford Studies in Ancient Philosophy* 2, 151–183.

Inwood, B. 1995. Review of Annas 1993. *Ancient Philosophy* 15 (2), 647–665.

Inwood, B. 1996. Review of Göransson 1995. *Bryn Mawr Classical Reviews* 7, 25–30.

Inwood, B. 2002. "Comments on White." Pp. 95–101 in *Eudaimonia and Well-Being: Ancient and Modern Conceptions* eds. L. J. Jost and R. A. Shiner = *Apeiron* 35.

Inwood, B. 2005. *Reading Seneca: Stoic Philosophy at Rome.* Oxford: Oxford University Press.

Inwood, B. 2007. "Moral Causes: The Role of Physical Explanations in Ancient Ethics." Pp. 14–36 in *Thinking about Causes: From Greek Philosophy to Modern Physics*, eds. Peter Machamer and Gereon Wolters. Pittsburgh: University of Pittsburgh Press.

Inwood, B. 2007a. *Seneca: Selected Philosophical Letters*. Oxford: Oxford University Press.

Inwood, B. 2007b. "The Importance of Form in Seneca's Philosophical Letters." Pp. 133–148 in *Ancient Letters: Classical and Late Antique Epistolography*, eds. Ruth Morello and A. D. Morrison. Oxford: Oxford University Press.

Inwood, B. 2014. "*Tria Genera Bonorum*." Pp. 255–280 in *Strategies of Argument: Essays in Ancient Ethics, Epistemology and Logic in Honor of Gisela Striker*, eds. M. Lee and M. Schiefsky. Oxford: Oxford University Press.

Inwood, B. forthcoming. "A Later (and Non-Standard) Aristotelian Account of Moral Motivation." In *Moral Motivation: A History*, ed. I. Vasiliou. Oxford: Oxford University Press.

Inwood, B., and J. Mansfeld. 1997. *Assent and Argument: Studies in Cicero's Academic Books*. Leiden: Brill.

Inwood, B., and R. Woolf. 2013. *Aristotle: Eudemian Ethics*. Cambridge: Cambridge University Press.

Ioppolo, A. M., and D. Sedley. 2007. *Pyrrhonists, Patricians, Platonizers: Hellenistic Philosophy in the Period 155–86 BC*. Naples: Bibliopolis.

Karamanolis, G. E. 2006. *Plato and Aristotle in Agreement? Platonists on Aristotle from Antiochus to Porphyry*. Oxford: Oxford University Press.

Kenny, A. 1978. *The Aristotelian Ethics*. Oxford: Oxford University Press.

Kraut, R., ed. 2006. *The Blackwell Guide to Aristotle's Nicomachean Ethics*. Oxford: Blackwell.

Laks, A., and G. Most, eds. 1993. *Théophraste: Métaphysique*. Paris: Les Belles Lettres.

Lennox, J. 1994. "The Disappearance of Aristotle's Biology: A Hellenistic Mystery." Pp. 7–24 in *The Sciences in Greco-Roman Society*, ed. T. D. Barnes = *Apeiron* 27.4.

Long, A. 2002. *Epictetus: A Stoic and Socratic Guide to Life*. Oxford: Oxford University Press.

Lynch, J. 1972. *Aristotle's School: A Study of a Greek Educational Institution*. Berkeley: University of California Press.

Matelli, E. 2004. "Hieronymus in Athens and Rhodes." Pp. 289–314 in Fortenbaugh and White 2004.

McConnell, S. 2012. "Cicero and Dicaearchus." *Oxford Studies in Ancient Philosophy* 42, 307–349.

153

McDowell, J. 1996. "Deliberation and Moral Development in Aristotle's Ethics." Pp. 19–35 in *Aristotle, Kant and the Stoics*, eds. S. Engstrom and J. Whiting. New York: Cambridge University Press.

McDowell, J. 1998. *Mind, Value, and Reality*. Cambridge, MA: Harvard University Press.

MacIntyre, A. 1981. *After Virtue: A Study in Moral Theory*. Notre Dame, IN: University of Notre Dame Press.

Mejer, J. 2004. "The Life of Lyco and the Life of the Lyceum." Pp. 277–287 in Fortenbaugh and White 2004.

Miller, J., ed. 2012. *The Reception of Aristotle's Ethics*. Cambridge: Cambridge University Press.

Moraux, P. 1973–2001. *Der Aristotelismus bei den Griechen*. 3 volumes. Berlin: De Gruyter.

Moss, J. 2012. *Aristotle on the Apparent Good*. Oxford: Oxford University Press.

Nehamas, A. 2010. "Aristotelian *philia*, Modern Friendship?" *Oxford Studies in Ancient Philosophy* 39, 213–247.

Nielsen, K. 2012. "The Nicomachean Ethics in Hellenistic Philosophy: A Hidden Treasure." Pp. 5–30 in Miller 2012.

Nussbaum, M. 1994. *The Therapy of Desire: Theory and Practice in Hellenistic Ethics*. Princeton, NJ: Princeton University Press.

Oliver, J. H. 1977. "The Diadoche at Athens under the Humanistic Emperors." *American Journal of Philology* 98, 160–178.

Oliver, J. H. 1983. *The Civic Tradition and Roman Athens*. Baltimore, MD: The Johns Hopkins University Press.

Owen, G. E. L. 1971–1972. "Aristotelian Pleasures." *Proceedings of the Aristotelian Society* 72, 135–152. Republished as ch. 19 of his collected papers, *Logic, Science and Dialectic*, ed. M. C. Nussbaum. Ithaca: Cornell University Press 1986.

Powell, J. G. F., ed. 1995. *Cicero the Philosopher*. Oxford: Oxford University Press.

Russell, D. 2010. "Virtue and Happiness in the Lyceum and Beyond." *Oxford Studies in Ancient Philosophy* 38, 143–185.

Russell, D. 2012. "Aristotle's Virtues of Greatness." Pp. 115–147 in *Virtue and Happiness: Essays in Honour of Julia Annas*, ed. R. Kamtekar (= *Oxford Studies in Ancient Philosophy*, supplementary volume 2012).

Schofield, M., ed. 2013. *Aristotle, Plato, and Pythagoreanism in the First Century BC: New Directions for Philosophy*. Cambridge: Cambridge University Press.

Schofield, M., and G. Striker. 1986. *The Norms of Nature: Studies in Hellenistic Ethics.* Cambridge and Paris: Cambridge University Press and Éditions de la Maison des Sciences de l'Homme.

Sedley, David. 1989. "Philosophical Allegiance in the Greco-Roman World," ch. 6 in Barnes and Griffin 1989.

Sedley, D. 2007. *Creationism and Its Critics in Antiquity.* Berkeley: University of California Press.

Sharples, R. 1983. "The Peripatetic Classification of Goods." Pp. 139–159 in Fortenbaugh 1983.

Sharples, R. 1987. "Alexander of Aphrodisias: Scholasticism and Innovation." Pp. 1176–1243 in *Aufstieg und Niedergang der Römischen Welt* (ed. H. Temporini and W. Haase; De Gruyter: Berlin and New York) ii.36.2.

Sharples, R. 1990. "The School of Alexander?" ch. 4 in Sorabji 1990.

Sharples, R. 1990a. *Alexander of Aphrodisias: Ethical Problems.* Ithaca, NY: Cornell University Press.

Sharples, R. 1992. *Alexander of Aphrodisias: Quaestiones 1.1–2.15.* Ithaca, NY: Cornell University Press.

Sharples, R. 1994. *Alexander of Aphrodisias: Quaestiones 2.16–3.15.* Ithaca, NY: Cornell University Press.

Sharples, R. 2002. "Aristotelian Theology after Aristotle." Pp. 1–40 in Frede and Laks 2002.

Sharples, R. 2004. *Alexander of Aphrodisias: Supplement to On the Soul.* Ithaca, NY: Cornell University Press.

Sharples, R. 2007. "Aristotle's Exoteric and Esoteric Works: Summaries and Commentaries," ch. 26 in Sharples and Sorabji 2007.

Sharples, R. 2007a. "Peripatetics on Happiness," ch. 35 in Sharples and Sorabji 2007.

Sharples, R. 2008 *Alexander of Aphrodisias, De anima libri mantissa.* Berlin: De Gruyter.

Sharples, R. 2010. *Peripatetic Philosophy 200 BC to 200 AD: An Introduction and Collection of Sources in Translation.* Cambridge: Cambridge University Press.

Sharples, R. 2010a. "Peripatetics," ch. 8 in *Cambridge History of Philosophy in Later Antiquity*, volume I, ed. L. P. Gerson. Cambridge: Cambridge University Press.

Sharples, R., and R. Sorabji, eds. 2007. *Greek and Roman Philosophy 100 BC–200 AD* (in two volumes = *Bulletin of the Institute of Classical Studies Supplement* 94). London: Institute of Classical Studies, University of London.

Sorabji, R. ed. 1990 *Aristotle Transformed: The Ancient Commentators and Their influence.* Ithaca, NY: Cornell University Press.

Sorabji, R. 2007. "Peripatetics on Emotion after 100 BC," ch. 34 in Sharples and Sorabji 2007.

Striker, G. 1986. "Antipater, or the Art of Living." Pp. 185–204 of Schofield and Striker 1986.

Striker, G. 1996. *Essays on Hellenistic Epistemology and Ethics.* Cambridge: Cambridge University Press.

Szaif, J. 2012. *Gut des Menschen: Untersuchungen zur Problematik und Entwicklung der Glücksethik bei Aristoteles und in der Tradition des Peripatos.* Berlin: De Gruyter.

Thompson, M. 2008. *Life and Action: Elementary Structures of Practice and Practical Thought.* Cambridge, MA: Harvard University Press.

Todd, R. B. 1976. *Alexander of Aphrodisias on Stoic Physics.* Leiden: Brill.

Trapp, M. 2007. *Philosophy in the Roman Empire: Ethics, Politics, and Society.* Aldershot, UK: Ashgate.

Tsouni, G. 2010. *Antiochus and Peripatetic Ethics.* Dissertation, Cambridge University.

Van der Eijk, P. 2009. "Aristotle! What a Thing for You to Say!" Pp. 261–281 in *Galen and the World of Knowledge,* eds. Christopher Gill, Tim Whitmarsh, and John Wilkins. Cambridge: Cambridge University Press.

Van Hoof, L. 2010. *Plutarch's Practical Ethics.* Oxford: Oxford University Press.

Wachsmuth, C. ed. 1884. *Ioannis Stobaei Anthologii Libri Duo Priores voll. I, II.* Reprint 1974, Dublin/Zürich: Weidmann.

Wehrli, F. 1967. *Die Schule des Aristoteles: Texte und Kommentar,* 2nd ed. Basel: Schwabe.

White, S. 1992. *Sovereign Virtue: Aristotle on the Relation between Happiness and Prosperity.* Stanford, CA: Stanford University Press.

White, S. 2002. "Happiness in the Hellenistic Lyceum." Pp. 69–93 in *Eudaimonia and Well-Being: Ancient and Modern Conceptions* eds. L. J. Jost and R. A. Shiner = *Apeiron* 35.

White, S. 2004. "Hieronymus of Rhodes: the Sources, Text and Translation." Pp. 79–276 in Fortenbaugh and White 2004.

Whiting, J. 2006. "The Nicomachean Account of *Philia*," ch. 13 in Kraut 2006.

Williams, B. 1985. *Ethics and the Limits of Philosophy.* Cambridge, MA: Harvard University Press.

Source Index

Alcinous

Didaskalikos

20–30, 32: 108

Alexander of Aphrodisias

Ethical Problems

118.23–120.2: 109–110

118.27: 111

119.4–5: 111

119.18–30: 111–112

119.30: 112

Mantissa

150–153: 109, 113–118

150.20: 120

150.27–28: 119

151.2–3: 119

151.3: 122

152.7–10: 120

152.15–24: 119

151.18: 122

151.30: 122

152.31–35: 121

153.16–21: 123

Aristotle

De Anima

I.3: 97

Nicomachean Ethics

I.7: 7, 10, 20, 80

I.13: 24, 79

7: 19

6: 19

8: 122

9: 112

10: 19, 40, 81, 122

1094a: 9

1100b22–1101a8: 35

1102a26–27: 25

1103b26–31: 31

1112a15–17: 32

1153b7–13: 19

1155b17–26: 114

1168a35–b10: 114

1175a10–17: 125

1175a18–21: 19

1176b26: 116

1177b3: 81

Eudemian Ethics
  1.1: 79
  6: 19
  7: 112
  8: 27
  8.2: 35
  1247b18–28: 36

[Aristotle]
Magna Moralia
  1.34.31: 27
  2.7: 32, 33
  2.8.1: 34
  1182a26–30: 32
  1182b3–4: 38
  1189a13–16: 32
  1189b16–17: 32
  1190a5–7: 32
  1191b25–29: 31
  1197b28–35: 31
  1198b4–8: 32
  1200a30–32: 33
  1205a26–b13: 33
  1206b17–29: 34
  1206b33–34: 34
  1208a31–b2: 30–31

[Arius Didymus]
Doxography C
  ap. Stobaeum *Ecl.* 2.7.13, pp.
    116–117 W: 78
  ap. Stobaeum *Ecl.* 2.7.13, pp.
    117–118 W: 79
  ap. Stobaeum *Ecl.* 2.7.13, pp.
    118–119 W: 79, 83–84
  ap. Stobaeum *Ecl.* 2.7.14, pp.
    126–127 W: 56–57, 138

  ap. Stobaeum *Ecl.* 2.7.20, p. 137:
    79

Cicero
Academica
  2.135: 91
On Goals
  3: 66, 87
  3.21–23: 87
  5: 17, 66, 67, 70–71, 79, 82, 101,
    109
  5.8: 71
  5.9: 67
  5.14: 71
  5.16–23: 67
  5.24: 67
  5.25–26: 67
  5.33: 68
  5.35: 68
  5.36: 68, 70
  5.39: 68
  5.45: 70
  5.48: 68, 70
  5.50–52: 70
  5.54–58: 68–70
  5.55: 69
  5.56: 69
  5.57: 69
  5.60: 70
  5.72: 62, 65, 70
  5.75: 72
De Oratore
  2.189 ff.: 92
Tusculan Disputations
  4: 93
  4.21: 93
  4.38: 94

4.43: 94
4.44: 95
4.45–46: 95
4.48–55: 95
4.55–56: 95
4.79: 96
Orator
128 ff.: 92

Chrysippus
Stoicorum veterum fragmenta, 3.12–15:
52

Critolaus
fr. 15: 53
fr. 19: 56
fr. 20: 55
fr 21: 60
fr. 24: 54
18N Sharples = Cicero *Tusculan Disputations* 5.75–76: 61

Diogenes Laërtius
Lives of the Philosophers
7.113: 93

Diogenes of Babylon
Stoicorum veterum fragmenta, 3.44–46: 52

Antipater
Stoicorum veterum fragmenta, 3.53: 57
3.57–58: 52

Hieronymus
fr. 6: 42
fr.11: 43
fr. 12: 42

fr. 13A: 43
fr. 16C: 43
fr. 22: 43
fr. 24: 42

Homer
Iliad
8.68–78: 58
22.208–213: 58

Horace
Ars Poetica
99ff.: 92

Lycon
fr. 10: 39

Plato
Euthydemus
278c: 57
281–282: 57
Meno
87–89: 57
Protagoras
356b: 59
Republic
7: 23
Symposium
205a1: 57

Plutarch
On Moral Virtue
440de: 106
442bc: 107
ch.6: 107

Theophrastus
fr. 440A: 25

fr. 440B: 26
fr. 440C: 26
fr. 441: 25
fr. 449A: 26
fr. 461: 27
fr. 493: 28
491: 28
492–500: 28

Pseudo-Andronicus
Peri Pathōn
4: 94

Seneca
De Ira
1.5: 97
1.6: 97
1.6.4: 97
1.6.5: 97
1.7.1: 98
1.9.1: 98
1.9.2: 98
1.12: 98

1.12.3: 99
1.12.6: 100
1.14.1: 99
1.17.1: 99
1.19.3: 99
1.19.7: 99
2: 100
2.14: 100
2.17: 100
3.3.1: 99
Letter 85: 103
Letter 87: 103
Letter 76: 103
Natural Questions
7: 89

Stobaeus
Anthology
2: 77
2.7: 93

Strato
fr. 134: 38

Subject Index

Academy, 14, 42–43, 49, 51, 53, 61–63,
  66, 71, 82, 89–91, 97–98, 102–104,
  113, 128, 137
action (*praxis*), 31, 40, 42, 57, 84, 94
activity (*energeia*), 5, 9–10, 15, 19–21, 32,
  35, 38, 40, 44, 46, 55–58, 60, 63–64,
  66, 69–70, 80–82, 84, 109–110,
  115–117, 123–125, 134, 137
actuality, 21, 38, 54–55, 84, 86,
  109–111, 121, 142
Adrastus, 130
Aenesidemus, 89
Alcinous, 17, 71, 75, 104, 108, 140
Alexander of Aphrodisias, 14–15, 17–18,
  48, 50, 73–75, 77, 79, 83, 104, 106,
  108–112, 118–125, 141, 144–146
Algra, K., 64
alignment condition, 118–120, 124, 145
Anaxagoras, 32
Andronicus of Rhodes, 76, 91, 105
anger, 26, 91–102, 142
animals, 7, 9–11, 19, 33, 40–41, 64–68,
  79–85, 110, 113, 118, 120–121,
  128, 145

Annas, J., 14, 20, 46, 64, 127–128
Anscombe, G.E.M., 3–4, 127
Antiochus of Ascalon, 16, 39, 43–44, 48,
  53, 56, 61, 63, 67, 71–72, 74, 82, 90,
  97, 103, 104, 110, 119, 135, 137, 139
Antipater of Tarsus, 51–54, 57, 63
appropriate action (*kathēkon*), 84
Arcesilaus, 42, 51, 134
argument on both sides of the question,
  54
Arius Didymus, 77–78, 129
Aspasius, 17, 75, 106–108, 131, 138
Atticus, 17, 75, 108
Augustus Caesar, 77

Barnes, J., 129
being, 1, 83, 109, 111, 114
biology, 1, 3, 7, 20–21, 64–65, 79, 88,
  138
blessed (*makarios*), 35
body, 21, 25–26, 28, 38, 54–56, 83–84,
  86–87, 106, 134, 141–142
body-soul relationship, 24–26, 54, 83,
  131, 141, 142

Boethus, 114, 122, 146
botany, 2, 29, 67
Burnyeat, M., 51

Callicles, 9
capacity (*dunamis*), 10, 19–21, 25, 38–40, 42, 64, 68, 80, 82, 84, 86, 110–112, 115, 120–121, 137, 142
Carneadea divisio, 43–44, 63, 64, 66
Carneades, 44, 49, 51, 53–54, 58, 64, 67, 118, 124, 145
Cato, 52, 67, 87
change (*kinēsis*), 32
character (*ethos*), 79
choice. *See prohairesis.*
Christianity, 12
Chrysippus, 42, 45, 47, 52, 96, 107, 135–136
Cicero, 15–17, 28, 35–36, 39, 43–44, 47–49, 53–54, 60–62, 64, 66, 71–73, 77, 82, 88–103, 109, 118, 129, 130, 133–135, 139
Clearchus, 16
Clement, 43, 52, 55, 134
Colotes, 47
commentary, 17, 75, 90, 104–108, 140
community, 85
consequentialism, 3, 13, 32, 60
contemplation (*theōria*), 12, 22–24, 27, 31, 45–46, 88, 123, 132
convention (*nomos*), 66, 81
correct action (*kathorthoun*), 36, 84
cosmology, 1, 53, 64, 105
cosmos, 29, 52–53, 110
courage, 8–9, 91, 98
cradle argument, 64, 66–67, 69, 77, 82, 85

craft (*technē*), 35, 54, 111, 123–124, 137
Crantor, 91, 98, 101–102
Critolaus, 16, 48–51, 53–58, 60, 62–63, 65–66, 70–72, 74, 82, 110, 129, 133, 137–139
culture, 8–9
Cynicism, 66, 89

deliberation, 12, 33, 89
Democritean tradition, 46–47
Democritus, 25, 131
deontology, 3, 4
desires, 25, 33, 65, 69, 83, 85–87, 93, 95, 110–111, 113–120, 123, 125
Dicaearchus, 45
Dillon, J. M., 131
Diodorus the Renegade (Stoic), 44
Diodorus of Tyre (Peripatetic), 71
Diogenes Laërtius, 93, 136, 145
Diogenes of Bablyon, 49, 51–53
dispositions, 22, 39, 137
disturbance, freedom from (*aochlēsia*), 42–44, 113, 135
doctrine of the mean, 91, 100, 107
doing well (*eupragia*), 35
doxography, 17, 56, 77, 107, 134, 138, 140, 144
Doxography C, 17, 77–78, 105, 109, 138, 140–141, 144
dualism, 25–26, 131

endearment (*oikeiōsis*), 64, 79, 83, 85–87, 111, 138, 140
endoxa (views of the many and the wise), 10, 20, 25, 41, 85
Epictetus, 74, 104

Epicurean(s), 11, 14, 19, 37, 41, 44–49, 58, 66, 77, 85, 90, 113, 119, 121–123, 136

Epicurus, 43–45, 47, 59, 61, 66, 135, 136

Epiphanius, 53

epistemology, 1, 51, 145

Eudemus, 45, 128, 132

Eudoxus, 40, 45, 65, 125

external goods, 21, 23–24, 27–28, 34, 38, 42, 54–57, 59, 61–62, 64, 72

Falcon, A., 76

filling (out) (*sumplērōsis*), 57, 59, 60, 137

fine (*kalon*), 33, 34–35, 39, 40–41, 54, 63–64, 114, 134

Foot, P., 7, 128

form (*eidos*), 104, 106–107, 141, 146

Fortenbaugh, W. W., 129–130

fortune and luck, 21–22, 24, 27–28, 34–36, 61–62, 72, 82, 111, 134

Frede, M., 129

friendship, 4–5, 12, 24, 88, 99, 114, 132

function (*ergon*), 7, 10, 68, 70, 79, 80

function argument, 7, 20, 64

generosity, 9

Gigante, M., 47

Gill, C., 127

Glibert-Thirry, A., 93

goal (*telos*), 7, 9, 15, 19–21, 29, 39–44, 51–52, 55–58, 63–64, 66, 74, 80, 82, 111, 115–120, 123–124, 135, 137, 145

god, 2, 10, 20–21, 29, 37–38, 41, 52–53, 61–62, 69, 80–84, 123–124, 132, 143

goods, 5, 8, 15, 21, 23, 27–28, 32, 38, 42, 52, 55–65, 67, 70–72, 74, 83, 86–87, 91, 103, 109–110, 112, 114–117, 119, 121–122, 138

Gottschalk, H., 14, 74–75

gratitude (*charis*), 24

greatness of soul (*megalopsuchia, magnitudo animi*), 35, 100, 134

happiness (*eudaimonia*), 4–7, 10, 13–14, 18, 20–24, 27–28, 31, 33, 35–39, 41–42, 45, 47, 52, 55, 57–63, 65, 70, 72, 80, 82, 103, 113, 116, 119, 131, 137, 139

"Harry" (author of Doxography C), 77–78, 83, 85–88, 104–105, 109–110, 120, 141

hedonism, 14–15, 19, 23, 32, 39–41, 44–45, 47, 65–66, 125, 128, 130, 133, 135

Heraclides Ponticus, 16, 134

Hermarchus, 47

Hieronymus of Rhodes, 16, 33, 42–46, 71, 99, 129, 133, 135–136

honor, 10

Horace, 92

human nature, 9–11, 20–21, 31, 33, 47, 59, 68, 81, 83, 100, 106, 110, 120, 123, 144

Hursthouse, R., 4–5

hylomorphism, 24–25, 28, 106, 131, 142

impulse (*hormē*), 79, 84

in our own power (*eph' hēmin*), 34

indifferents, 109–110

instrumentalism, 27, 42, 87

intellect (*nous*), 19, 69, 82, 115, 120, 142, 145
intellectual virtues, 21, 32
intellectualism, 32
intuition, 60, 80

joy (*chara*), 39

Kallipolis, 23
Kant, 13
Kant(ian), 3, 12–13
Kenny, A., 129
knowledge (*epistēmē*), 10, 31, 33, 67–68, 95

life, its status as a good, 109–112, 115, 117–118, 125
logic, 3

Lyceum, 128
Lycon, 16, 39–42, 44–46, 129, 133–134
Lynch, J., 128

Magna Moralia, 16, 26–27, 30, 35–38, 40, 76–79, 132, 138
"Magnus" (author of *Magna Moralia*), 30–33, 36, 38–39, 132–133
Marcus Aurelius, 48
matter (*hulē*), 53, 104, 106–107, 141
McDowell, J., 13
mean, 22, 26, 31, 33, 91, 94, 97, 100–101, 107
metaphysics, 1, 3, 7, 20, 38, 74, 142, 145
moderation, 22, 26, 92
moral psychology, 5, 12, 25, 106
Moraux, P., 14, 74–75, 127
Moss, J., 130

motivation, 41, 85–88, 119, 122

natural inclination, 34, 36
natural philosophy, 1, 16, 37, 41, 67, 70
natural world, 7, 9, 19–20, 40–41, 68
naturalism, 6–11, 18–21, 25, 27, 37–38, 52, 62, 64–68, 70, 72, 77, 79–82, 88, 106, 109, 112, 122–125, 128, 133
nature (*phusis*), 6–10, 21, 33, 37, 41, 52–53, 58, 62, 64, 66–67, 69–70, 79, 81, 83–87, 94–98, 100–102, 109–111, 115, 117, 121, 123–124, 141, 146
Neo-Aristotelianism, 4–5, 11, 46, 88, 124
nonnaturalist theories, 7–8, 80

Owen, G. E. L., 130

pain, 33, 43–44, 58, 64, 86, 91, 95, 131, 142
parts of the soul, 21, 25, 36, 52, 76, 79, 84, 107
passion (*pathos*), 17, 22–26, 31, 33, 54, 74–76, 78, 88–92, 94–98, 101–106, 108, 130–132, 142
passion, freedom from (*apatheia*), 91, 101, 131
passion, moderated (*metriopatheia*), 26, 31, 91, 101, 143
perception, 25, 116
Peripatetic(s) (ancient Aristotelians), 6, 14–17, 26, 30, 33, 35–37, 40–46, 48–51, 53, 55–57, 61–62, 65–68, 71–79, 82–83, 85–86, 88–106, 108, 110–113, 116, 119, 121–122, 124, 127–129, 131, 134–135, 138, 139–140, 143–146

Philo of Larissa, 89

Philopator, 109

physicalism, 28

physics, 3, 16, 38, 45, 47, 53, 74, 77, 109, 112

Piso, 43, 62, 66–68, 70–72, 82–83, 85, 110, 119–120, 124, 139

Plato, 2, 12, 16, 19, 20, 22, 25, 46, 54, 59, 63, 66, 76–77, 90–91, 97, 99, 107, 136, 143

Platonism, 3, 14, 17–18, 23, 32, 49, 57, 71, 74–76, 81, 89–90, 98, 103–104, 106–108, 123–124, 140, 142

pleasure, 10, 18–19, 24, 32–33, 37, 39–42, 44, 47, 58–60, 64, 69, 70, 75, 83–84, 88, 113–118, 120–121, 123, 125, 130–131, 132, 134, 136, 145

Plotinus, 48, 75

Plutarch, 17, 25–26, 47–48, 71, 75–76, 104, 106–108, 134–135, 137

political science (*politikē*), 3, 23–24, 31, 49

Posidonius, 52

potentiality. *See* capacity

practical vs theoretical life, 22–24, 31–32, 45–46, 69, 88, 135–136

practical wisdom (*phronēsis*), 4–5, 12, 22, 26–27, 32, 86–87, 89

Priam, 21, 35

primary object of attachment (*prōton oikeion*), 113–119, 121–122, 146

principle (*archē*), 32, 34, 53, 88

prohairesis (choice), 32, 74, 104

providence (*pronoia*), 53, 124, 146

psychology, 1, 3, 102

punishment, 8, 93, 99

Pyrrhonism, 89

Pythagoreans, 89

quietism, 44–46, 136

quintessence (*aithēr*), 54

reason (*logos*), 22, 28, 31, 33–34, 76, 78–79, 81–82, 86–87, 106, 110, 117, 123, 132

relativism, 11, 80

rhetoric, 1, 53–54, 91–92, 137

sciences, 23, 25, 38

self-control, 107

self-love, 66

self-preservation, 66, 110, 112

Seneca, 48, 74, 88–93, 97–105, 136, 143–144

Sextius and the Sextii, 89

Sextus Empiricus, 89

Sharples, R., 14, 56, 74–75, 111, 127, 129

skepticism, 49, 51, 62, 82, 90

smooth flow of life (*eurrhoia tou biou*), 55

social, society, etc., 11, 20–21, 24, 85

sociobiology, 9

Socrates, 23, 32, 46, 54

Socratic schools, 96–97

Sosicrates, 106, 115, 122, 145–146

soul, 10, 24–26, 38–39, 52–56, 59–61, 68, 83–84, 86–87, 107, 109, 134, 137, 141–142

specialness of human beings, 10, 20, 41, 124, 128

starting point. *See* principle

Staseas of Naples, 71–72, 139

Stobaeus, 77, 93, 129, 138

Stoics, 11–12, 14, 17–18, 27, 31, 35–37, 39, 41–42, 44–47, 49, 51–58, 60–62, 64, 66–68, 72, 74, 76–77, 79, 81–82, 84–88, 90–95, 97, 100–113, 119, 121–123, 129, 130–131, 134, 137–138, 143–144

Strato of Lampsacus, 16, 37–39, 42, 45, 128, 133, 135

strength of will (*enkrateia*), 25

Striker, G., 51, 64, 118, 144

summum bonum, 15

supernaturalism, 80, 123

Szaif, J., 127, 129

teleology, 2, 7–8, 11, 20, 68, 79, 81, 86, 88, 94–96, 100–102, 110, 112, 120, 122, 124, 128, 145

theology, 2, 8, 52, 81, 110, 123

Theophrastus, 14–16, 24–25, 27–30, 32, 34, 36–38, 45, 61–62, 72, 82, 93, 99, 128, 130–132, 135, 138–139

theoretical life. *See* practical vs theoretical life

theoretical philosophy, 32

theoretical wisdom (*sophia*), 26–27, 31–32

Thomas Aquinas, 6

Thompson, M., 7

thought, 25

tria genera bonorum, 38, 54, 61, 70, 103

Tsouni, G., 138

utilitarianism, 4, 12

utility, 6, 70, 96, 132

Verginius Rufus, 106, 115, 122, 145–146

Virtue (*aretê*), 4–7, 10–13, 15, 20, 22, 24, 27, 33, 35–37, 39, 41–43, 47, 54–57, 59–62, 72, 79, 82, 84, 86–88, 91, 94, 103, 106–108, 110, 117, 119, 124–125, 131–132, 134–135, 142

Virtue ethics, 3, 6, 10–11, 13, 88, 124

voluntary , 12, 24

weakness of will (*akrasia*), 12, 22, 25

White, S., 38–39, 44–46, 60, 129, 134

Xenarchus of Seleucia, 76, 78, 105, 114, 122, 141, 146

Xenocrates, 17

Zeno of Citium, 42, 55, 107, 136

Zeno of Sidon, 47

zoology, 1, 67